Plant-Based Cookbook

The Ultimate Beginner's Guide to Delicious Vegan Cooking with Easy-to-Cook Flavorful Recipes and Colorful Pictures - Includes a Detailed 30-Day Meal Plan for Healthy Living

Grace Love

Table *of* CONTENTS

FOREWORD

Grace Love is a devoted supporter of a plant-based lifestyle. She has continuously explored and embraced this lifestyle for the past seven years. She found the amazing benefits of plant-based diets with her own health transformation, which ignited a spark and pushed her toward sharing the uncountable benefits of this eating plan with others in the shape of this valuable and comprehensive plant-based cookbook. Grace's personal journey and substantial research on plant-based living make her an expert on this subject.

Because Grace has been on this path herself, she is well aware of the obstacles and rewards that come with adopting a plant-based diet. Her unwavering dedication to advocating healthy living and viable eating habits has provided her with the expertise to help others accomplish their health goals. Grace composed this book to share her knowledge and encourage readers to switch to plant-based living, which she believes can bring about life-changing and transformative outcomes.

INTRODUCTION

I welcome you to a path that can change your life. Visualize this: an energetic, lively you getting out of bed every morning feeling fresh and ready to make the most of your day. Picture yourself eating meals that not only entice your taste buds but also provide important nutrients to your body, mind, and soul. This is the aim of a plant-based lifestyle, and this book will help you unlock all that it has to offer.

We are seeing an era of awakening, a time when most of us are breaking stereotypical beliefs and old patterns that are no longer beneficial for us. We are embracing new ideologies, ways of living, and ways of facing reality. For a few, this awakening means a change in their relationship with the food they consume.

This book is meant to assist and guide you on your journey toward health and happiness through delicious plant-based cooking. I myself experienced a spiritual awakening when I embraced a plant-based lifestyle. In my case, the transition was quite natural and without much hassle, partly because of religious fasting that restricted the consumption of animal products. Once the fasting period ended, I just did not want to eat animal products anymore. For me, this change was more about energizing my soul and creating a deeper connection with God than it was about changing my diet.

Going vegan and embracing a plant-based diet has healed me in many ways. The idea that "our diet shapes who we are" holds weight—opting for nourishing plant-based meals enhances our health, emotions, and spirituality. It truly uplifts our energy levels.

Many individuals face challenges when it comes to maintaining a diet. You may be tired of feeling low on energy or struggling with chronic health issues. You might have heard about the benefits of following a plant-based diet but feel overwhelmed by the thought of making such a change. The uncertainty surrounding what to eat, how to cook meals, and ensuring you meet all your nutrient needs can feel intimidating, but you are not alone.

This book aims to address those concerns. Each section is filled with suggestions, tasty recipes, and helpful advice tailored to help you smoothly transition to a plant-based way of life. Through step-by-step instructions, you'll gain the skills to prepare meals that are not just nutritious but also delicious and enjoyable.

Picture all the things that could happen: enhanced energy levels, improved digestion, clearer skin, and a stronger immune system.

Your relationship with food will transform as you realize the power of plants. It's not about changing what you eat; it's about improving your well-being and embracing a lifestyle that promotes long-term vitality and health.

I have personally walked down this path before. I faced my health challenges and tried different diets until I discovered the life-changing effects of plant-based eating.

My passion for plant-based living and my journey have given me insights and knowledge to support you. Together, we'll navigate this journey and unlock the benefits.

As you delve into these pages, you'll discover more than recipes. You'll gain an understanding of the core principles behind plant-based nutrition and how to incorporate them into your daily routine. This book serves as your guide to embracing a plant-based diet with happiness and confidence.

Are you ready to start this life-changing adventure?

Let's jump into Chapter 1 and start improving your life, one plant-based meal at a time.

Everything About Plant-Based Diet

Many individuals believe that following a plant-based diet involves consuming boring salads. Nonetheless, this belief is simply a misconception. While plant-based eating may include salads here and there, it is not limited to that. Plant-based diets consist of an array of foods, ranging from colorful fruits and vegetables to filling grains and legumes.

In this chapter, we will delve into the essence of a plant-based diet, highlighting its elements and demonstrating how this eating lifestyle offers both nutrition and pleasure.

What is a Plant-Based Diet?

A plant-based diet is pretty straightforward. It mainly involves consuming foods that come from plant sources, such as fruits, vegetables, nuts, seeds, whole grains, and legumes. This diet focuses on plant-based foods while limiting the consumption of animal-based products and fats. In essence, a plant-based diet revolves around plant sources for nutrition. Animal products like meat, eggs, honey, and dairy items are not a part of this eating approach. However, some variations can be in how people interpret the terms "plant-based" and "vegan." For instance, some individuals follow a flexitarian diet that allows small servings of meat or fish consumption but predominantly consists of vegetarian fare. Diets that omit meat but include fish are known as pescatarian diets; those excluding both meat and fish while incorporating eggs and dairy are referred to as vegetarian. People who refrain from all animal-derived items, like dairy products, honey, and gelatin, are termed vegans. Plant-based whole foods offer a mix of carbohydrates and fiber that contribute to maintaining body wellness.

Is It Healthy to Follow a Plant-Based Diet?

Absolutely. A plant-based diet is known

for being abundant in fiber, good fats, proteins, vitamins, and minerals. It is widely regarded as a healthy eating approach that can fulfill all your nutrient requirements.

Transitioning to a Plant-Based Diet

- Start Gradually.

Begin by slowly incorporating plant-based meals into your eating habits. Think about swapping out one meal per week with plant-based alternatives.

- Experiment with Different Recipes.

Explore new recipes and various cuisines to bring more excitement and flavors to your meals.

- Create a Balanced Plate.

Make sure to include a variety of food groups in each meal to meet your nutritional requirements.

Common Misconceptions About Plant-Based Diet

- Insufficient Protein.

Many people mistakenly believe that plant-based diets do not provide enough protein. Plenty of plant-based foods, like beans, tofu, lentils, and quinoa, are excellent protein sources.

- Expensive.

While some specialty plant-based products may be expensive, choosing simple diet-focused plant-based foods is cost-effective.

- Lack of Important Nutrients.

Some people think that plant-based diets lack essential nutrients like iron and calcium. However, leafy greens, tofu, tahini, and fortified plant milk are rich in Calcium, and legumes, nuts, grains, seeds, and green vegetables are rich in Iron.

- Hard to Maintain.

There is a misconception that sticking to a plant-based diet is too challenging and restrictive. With proper meal planning and access to various delicious plant-based recipes, following this lifestyle can be straightforward and enjoyable.

- Insufficient Physical Performance.

It is commonly believed that athletes struggle to achieve their performance while following a plant-based diet. Numerous accomplished athletes attribute their plant-based eating habits to faster recovery and better overall well-being.

- Sense of Isolation and Disconnection.

Some people think that following a plant-based diet can lead to difficulties in social situations. However, with the increasing acceptance of plant-based diets, many restaurants and social gatherings now offer a selection of plant-based dishes, making it easier for individuals to enjoy meals together. Eating a plant-based diet is good for your health and helps the environment. By choosing various nutrient-packed plant-based foods, you can create meals that support your well-being and minimize the impact on the planet.

The 5 Food Groups of a Plant-Based Diet

So...what can you even eat when following a plant-based diet?
Just like any other eating pattern, following a plant-based diet requires a balanced approach of incorporating foods from various sources and food groups to ensure our bodies receive all the essential vitamins, minerals, and nutrients for optimal health and function. It's essential to include a variety of foods in the correct quantities to meet our nutritional needs effectively on a plant-based diet.

I have experienced situations where I have tried restricting food groups, sticking to a couple of them, and not consuming adequate amounts from any of them. This approach could be more effective. Consequently, this is a factor that contributes to why some individuals feel that a plant-based diet is ineffective for them.

Research and various studies indicate that plant-based diets are not only nutritionally sufficient, but can also potentially prevent, manage, and even reverse common chronic illnesses and health issues. By incorporating plant-based foods into our diet, we can get optimal energy levels, maintain good skin, hair, and nails, manage weight effectively without strict limitations, promote strong bones, ensure hormonal balance, and enjoy many other health benefits.

Here is a helpful overview of the five plant-based food categories for a nourishing and well-rounded diet:

- **Vegetables**

We all know the benefits of vegetables! They are packed with vitamins, minerals, and antioxidants that protect us from diseases and keep our cells healthy. It's essential to have a variety of veggies on your plate, as different colors indicate different nutrients and health perks in these vegetables.

Most veggies are low in calories and high in nutrients, making them perfect for filling up your meals and keeping you satisfied.

Some of the veggies I love include carrots, spinach, broccoli, cauliflower, cucumbers, purple cabbage, kale, beets, sweet potatoes, tomatoes, eggplants, bell peppers, pumpkins, corn, and potatoes.

- **Fruits**

Contrary to popular belief, fruit is more than just sugar. While it does contain sugar, it also boasts a wealth of vitamins, phytochemicals, minerals, and fiber, much like vegetables! These components facilitate a consistent release of glucose into the bloodstream, offering energy and many health benefits. With its natural sweetness and rich flavor profile, fruit is an ideal snack and a wholesome natural sweetener for breakfast dishes, baked goods, smoothies, desserts, and other culinary creations. The optimal taste and digestion experience with fruit is achieved when it's in season and ripe!

My picks include bananas, oranges, mangoes, berries, peaches, nectarines, passion fruits, kiwis, persimmons, melons, apples, lime, and papaya.

- **Whole Grains**

I recommend incorporating grains into your meals because they provide a fantastic energy source. Their slow-digesting complex carbohydrates assist in keeping blood sugar and energy levels stable. Opting for whole grains is my go-to choice, as they offer a blend of fiber, minerals, vitamins, protein, and essential fatty acids compared to refined grains. Whether I cook them whole or use them as flour for baking, whole grains always make a great foundation for my dishes!
Some of the grains that I particularly like are oats, wheat, spelt, rye, barley, rice, buckwheat, millet, and quinoa. While the last three are technically seeds or 'pseudo-grains, they share properties similar to traditional grains, so I like to include them in this category too!

- **Legumes**

Legumes are often overlooked in our society, but they are truly remarkable! Beans, lentils, and other legumes provide an amazing source of plant protein, while fiber, vitamins, and minerals offer health benefits. They can help prevent chronic diseases, regulate blood sugar levels, support a healthy gut, and more. These foods are versatile, delicious, satisfying, and budget-friendly. Embrace the power of plants!
I enjoy transforming legumes into dips such as hummus or refried beans or whipping up bean chili, curries, dal, and lentil bolognese. They can also be tossed into salads and used to make sweet treats like black bean brownies or cookies. Additionally, soy products like tempeh and tofu provide another option within the legume family.
My top picks include chickpeas, black beans, lentils, kidney beans, split peas, butter beans, green peas, tempeh, and mung beans.

- **Nuts and Seeds**

Nuts and seeds are like powerhouses of nutrients and energy, full of vitamins, minerals, fiber, protein, and those essential fatty acids your body loves. Omega 3 fatty acids in nuts and seeds help fight inflammation and are super important for your brain, skin, hair, and hormone production. They are not just healthy but also add a lot of flavor and satisfaction to meals. You can snack on them or get creative by making raw cheesecakes, nut milk, cheeses, nut butter, and more. The possibilities are endless!
I really love chia seeds, almonds, flax seeds, hemp seeds, Brazil nuts, walnuts, cashews, pumpkin seeds, sunflower seeds, peanuts, and sesame seeds.
I hope this information has helped you understand the essentials of a nutritious plant-based diet. Let's move to the next chapter and explore its advantages.

Health Benefits of a Plant-Based Diet

Adopting a plant-based eating plan is not about altering what you eat; it involves a holistic method to enhance one's overall well-being and quality of life. There are various advantages to embracing this approach, such as experiencing improved wellness and fewer instances of illness. The idea that consuming plant-based foods can boost energy levels and promote health has been widely accepted for a considerable period. Individuals who follow this lifestyle also appear to exhibit more happiness and less irritation, leading to a smoother and more peaceful existence. Additionally, other benefits associated with this diet include:

- **Weight loss.** According to a study conducted in 2018, individuals on a plant-based diet were found to have weight loss results compared to those consuming meat. The research monitored participants following their regular diets & some following plant-based diets, revealing that the plant-based diet group shed nearly 15 lbs in just four months.

- **Reduces Risk of Heart Disease.** A study conducted in 2019 by the American Heart Association revealed that individuals who follow a plant-based diet have lower risks of heart disease. Additionally, this dietary choice is associated with a decreased likelihood of experiencing stroke, type 2 diabetes, high blood pressure, and obesity.

- **Diabetes Prevention.** It also improves insulin sensitivity in individuals with diabetes. Research conducted in 2009, engaging tens of thousands of participants, revealed that the percentage of plant-based food consumers who developed diabetes was 2.9% lower than that of meat eaters. A study released in 2018 indicated that diabetes shows improvement when adhering to a diet rich in plant-based foods.

- **Reduces Cholesterol.** Making eco-friendly choices can significantly reduce LDL cholesterol in your bloodstream - this type of cholesterol can lead to heart disease and stroke. Avoid margarine, skip fatty meats, and opt for plant-based foods instead. Dairy and processed foods are high in fat and lacking in fiber. Plant-based diets are entirely cholesterol-free.

- **Prevents the Likelihood of Cancer.** Eating a diet high in fat has been linked to an increased risk of cancer. Prioritizing fruits, vegetables, and other natural compounds helps prevent cancer.

This eating plan does not require any commitment or investment; individuals can start it whenever they choose. While many dieting trends demand investments for short-lived outcomes, this plant-based regimen has proven effective in achieving long-term, significant weight loss and health improvements for millions.

Basic Kitchen Equipment

Having the right cooking gear can simplify the process of making plant-based meals and make it more enjoyable. Here are some items worth considering:

- Good-Quality Knives: Essential for chopping vegetables and fruits.
- Blender or Food Processor: Useful for home smoothies, soups, and sauces.
- Chopping Boards: Having a few is good to prevent mixing foods.
- Non-Stick Pan: Ideal for cooking without oil.
- Steamer Basket: Great for steaming vegetables.
- Instant Pot or Pressure Cooker: Helps speed up the cooking time of grains and legumes.
- Storage Containers: Important for batch cooking and storing leftovers.

Batch Cooking

Cooking in batches can be a time saver and helps you have nutritious meals readily available. Here are a few suggestions to consider:

- Meal Planning: Figure out what dishes you'd like to prepare for the week.
- Bulk Cooking: Make large batches of beans, grains, and veggies in advance.
- Freeze Extra Portions: Store your meals in containers for freezing and reheating whenever you need them.

Stock Up on Plant-Based Foods

Consider stocking up on rice, bulgur, vegetables, canned beans, and fruits. You can also opt for frozen fruits to prevent wastage.

Storing Food

Properly storing plant-based foods is critical to keeping them fresh and minimizing waste. Here are some suggestions:

- Refrigerate Your Produce: Extend the lifespan of your fruits and veggies by storing them in the refrigerator.
- Opt for Airtight Containers: Preserve the freshness of nuts, grains, and seeds by using airtight containers.
- Mark with Labels and Dates: To keep track of what to use first, label and date your stored food items accordingly.
- Arrange Your Pantry Systematically: Make meal preparation more convenient by organizing ingredients.

Make it Enjoyable

Explore various plant-based foods after following a plant-based diet for weeks or months. Get creative by preparing vegan adaptations of your go-to dishes or trying a new recipe. Feel free to try recipes from this cookbook or look up new ideas online. Stroll through your grocery store's fruit and vegetable section to discover new fruits & veggies.

01

CHAPTER ONE

Morning Bliss Choices

Green Smoothie Bowl

SERVES 2

Ingredients

- [ ] 2 C. fresh spinach
- [ ] 1 medium avocado, peeled, pitted, and chopped roughly
- [ ] 2 scoops of unsweetened vegan protein powder
- [ ] 3 tbsp. maple syrup
- [ ] 2 tbsp. fresh lemon juice
- [ ] 1 C. unsweetened almond milk
- [ ] ¼ C. ice cubes

Directions

1. In a blender, add the spinach and remaining ingredients and process to form a smooth mixture.
2. Enjoy immediately with your favorite topping.

Granola & Berries Yogurt Bowl

SERVES 4

Ingredients

- [ ] ½ C. fresh blueberries
- [ ] ½ C. fresh raspberries
- [ ] 2½ C. coconut yogurt, divided
- [ ] ½ C. crunchy maple granola

Directions

1. In a bowl, blend berries.
2. In 4 serving bowls, divide the yogurt evenly.
3. Top with berries and granola, and enjoy immediately.

Chia Seed Pudding

SERVES 3

Ingredients

- [ ] 2 C. unsweetened almond milk
- [ ] ½ C. chia seeds
- [ ] 1 tbsp. maple syrup
- [ ] 1 tsp. vanilla extract

To serve

- [ ] ½ fresh berries
- [ ] A drizzle of honey

Directions

1. Add the almond milk, chia seeds, maple syrup, and vanilla extract into a large-sized bowl and blend to incorporate thoroughly.
2. Refrigerate for at least 3-4 hours, stirring occasionally.
3. Enjoy with your favorite berries topping, and drizzle on some extra honey.

Blueberry Oatmeal

SERVES 2

Ingredients

- [ ] 2 C. unsweetened almond milk
- [ ] 1 C. gluten-free oats
- [ ] ¼ C. frozen blueberries
- [ ] 2 tbsp. pure maple syrup
- [ ] 1 tbsp. fresh lemon juice

To serve

- [ ] 1 C. fresh blueberries
- [ ] 1 tsp ground cinnamon
- [ ] 1 tbsp. flaxseed

Directions

1. Put the almond milk, oats, and frozen blueberries into a pot over medium heat and cook for 5-7 minutes.
2. Remove the pot of oatmeal from the heat and add maple syrup and lemon juice.
3. Serve the oatmeal with fresh blueberries, cinnamon, and flaxseed.

Porridge with Berries & Seeds

SERVES 2

Ingredients

- [ ] ½ C. organic, gluten-free, rolled oats
- [ ] 1 cup coconut milk
- [ ] ½ C. filtered water
- [ ] 1 tsp. almond butter
- [ ] 2 tsp. seed mixture of ground flax seeds, pumpkin seeds, sunflower seeds
- [ ] 1 handful of berries of your choice
- [ ] ½ tsp. ground cinnamon
- [ ] ¼ tsp. ground ginger

Directions

1. In a small saucepan, combine the rolled oats with coconut milk and water and bring to a boil.
2. Reduce the temperature and simmer for about 10 minutes until it thickens. Stir constantly to prevent it from burning.
3. Add cinnamon and ground ginger.
4. Stir in the almond butter and top with berries and seeds.

Apple Cinnamon Oatmeal

SERVES 4

Ingredients

- [ ] 1 C. organic, gluten-free, rolled oats
- [ ] 2 C. unsweetened almond milk
- [ ] 3 tbsp. walnuts, chopped
- [ ] 3 tbsp. sunflower seeds
- [ ] 2 large apples, peeled, cored, and grated
- [ ] 1 tsp. maple syrup
- [ ] Pinch of ground cinnamon
- [ ] ½ small apple, cored and sliced

Directions

1. In a small saucepan, combine grated apples, maple syrup, cinnamon, and sauté for a few minutes. Set aside.
2. In a large pot, add the oats, milk, walnuts, and sunflower seeds over medium heat. Cook for about 5 minutes, stirring occasionally.
3. Transfer the porridge into serving bowls. Top with cinnamon apples.
4. Top with apple slices and enjoy.

Buckwheat Porridge

SERVES 2

Ingredients

- ☐ ½ C. buckwheat groats
- ☐ 2 tbsp. chia seeds
- ☐ 15-20 almonds
- ☐ 1 C. unsweetened almond milk
- ☐ ½ tsp. ground cinnamon
- ☐ 1 tsp. vanilla extract
- ☐ 3-4 drops liquid stevia

Directions

1. In a large bowl, soak buckwheat groats in 1 C. of water overnight. In 2 bowls, soak chia seeds & almonds separately.
2. Drain the buckwheat and rinse well.
3. Add the buckwheat and almond milk to a non-stick pot over medium heat and cook for 7 minutes or until creamy.
4. Drain the chia seeds and almonds well.
5. Take the pot from heat and blend in the almonds, chia seeds, cinnamon, vanilla extract, and stevia.
6. Enjoy warm with your favorite topping.

Spiced Quinoa Porridge

SERVES 4

Ingredients

- ☐ 2 C. water
- ☐ 1 C. dry quinoa, rinsed
- ☐ ½ tsp. vanilla extract
- ☐ ½ C. unsweetened almond milk
- ☐ 6 drops liquid stevia
- ☐ ¼ tsp. lemon peel, grated finely
- ☐ ½ tsp. ground ginger
- ☐ ½ tsp. ground cinnamon
- ☐ ½ tsp. ground nutmeg

Directions

1. Combine water, quinoa, and vanilla extract in a pot over low heat. Cook for 10-15 minutes, stirring occasionally.
2. Add the almond milk, stevia, lemon peel, and spices and blend to incorporate thoroughly.
3. Enjoy warm with your favorite topping.

16

BANANA
Muffins

 PREP 15 MIN   COOK 30 MIN    SERVES 6

Ingredients

- [ ] Non-stick baking spray
- [ ] 1 tbsp. flaxseed meal
- [ ] 2½ tbsp. water
- [ ] 1 C. whole-wheat flour
- [ ] 1 C. almond flour
- [ ] 1 tsp. baking soda
- [ ] 1 tsp. ground cinnamon
- [ ] 1/8 tsp. salt
- [ ] 4 bananas, peeled and mashed
- [ ] 1 C. unsweetened almond milk
- [ ] ½ C. coconut oil, melted
- [ ] 1 tsp. vanilla extract

Directions

1. Preheat your oven to 325°F. Grease a 12-cup muffin tin with baking spray.
2. In a large bowl, blend the flaxseed meal and water. Set aside for about 5 minutes.
3. Blend the flour, baking soda, cinnamon, and salt in a bowl.
4. In the bowl of flaxseed mixture, add the bananas, almond milk, coconut oil, and vanilla extract and whisk to incorporate thoroughly.
5. Add the flour mixture and gently blend to incorporate.
6. Place the mixture into the muffin cups.
7. Bake for about 25-30 minutes.
8. Remove the muffin tin from the oven and place it on a wire rack for 10 minutes.
9. Carefully invert the muffins onto the wire rack to cool completely before enjoying.

APPLE & DATE
Cookies

 PREP 15 MIN  COOK 15 MIN  SERVES 8

Ingredients

- ☐ Non-stick baking spray
- ☐ ¼ C. old-fashioned oats
- ☐ 8 large dates, pitted
- ☐ 1/3 C. unsweetened applesauce
- ☐ 1/2 C. peanut butter (nut butter)
- ☐ ½ tsp. ground ginger
- ☐ ½ tbsp. ground cinnamon
- ☐ 1/2 C. nuts, seeds, dried berries mix
- ☐ 2 tbsp. flaxseed meal
- ☐ 2 tsp. vanilla extract
- ☐ 1 tsp. baking powder
- ☐ ¼ tsp. salt
- ☐ 1 medium apple, peeled, cored and chopped

Directions

1. Preheat your oven to 350°F. Grease a large cookie sheet with baking spray.
2. Combine dried oatmeal, applesauce, chopped dates, nuts and seeds, cinnamon, peanut butter, and other ingredients.
3. Roll the applesauce cookie dough into 8 balls, each about 2 inches in size. Press and shape them into cookie forms, then arrange them on a cookie sheet.
4. Bake for about 15 minutes or until the edges feel firm to the touch.
5. Take off from oven and place the cookie sheet onto a wire rack for about 5 minutes to rest.
6. Enjoy.

Zucchini Bread

SERVES 6

Ingredients

- [ ] Non-stick baking spray
- [ ] ½ C. almond flour, sifted
- [ ] 1½ tsp. baking soda
- [ ] ½ tsp. ground cinnamon
- [ ] 1½ C. banana, peeled and mashed
- [ ] ¼ C. almond butter, softened
- [ ] 2 tsp. vanilla extract
- [ ] 1 C. zucchini, shredded

Directions

1. Preheat your oven to 350°F. Grease a loaf pan with baking spray.
2. Blend the flour, baking soda, and cinnamon in a large bowl.
3. Mix banana, almond butter, and vanilla in another bowl. Add the zucchini and fold to combine.
4. Add the dry ingredients to the wet ingredients and mix.
5. Transfer the batter to the loaf pan.
6. Bake for about 40-45 minutes.
7. Take it out from the oven and let it rest for 10 minutes before serving.

Mushroom & Avocado Toast

SERVES 2

Ingredients

- [ ] 1-2 tbsp. olive oil
- [ ] 3 C. fresh mushrooms, sliced
- [ ] ½ tsp. dried thyme
- [ ] Salt and ground black pepper, as desired
- [ ] 2 vegan bread slices, toasted
- [ ] ½ of medium ripe avocado, peeled, pitted, and mashed
- [ ] pinch of microgreens

Directions

1. Heat oil in a large wok over medium heat. Add the mushrooms and thyme and cook for 5-7 minutes, stirring occasionally.
2. Add salt and pepper and take off from the heat.
3. Spread mashed avocado over each bread slice.
4. Top with mushrooms, and microgreens and enjoy.

MATCHA
Pancakes

 PREP 15 MIN  COOK 24 MIN SERVES 6

Ingredients

- [ ] 2 tbsp. flaxseed meal
- [ ] 5 tbsp. warm water
- [ ] 1 C. spelt flour
- [ ] 1 C. buckwheat flour
- [ ] 1 tbsp. matcha powder
- [ ] 1 tbsp. baking powder

- [ ] Pinch of salt
- [ ] ¾ C. unsweetened almond milk
- [ ] 1 tbsp. olive oil
- [ ] 1 tsp. vanilla extract
- [ ] Non-stick baking spray
- [ ] 1/3 C. maple syrup

Directions

1. In a bowl, blend the flaxseed meal and warm water. Set aside for 5 minutes.
2. Add the almond milk, oil, vanilla extract and whisk to incorporate thoroughly.
3. In another bowl, place the flour, matcha powder, baking powder, and salt and blend thoroughly.
4. Now, mix them together and blend to form a smooth mixture.
5. Lightly grease a non-stick wok with baking spray and heat over medium-high heat.
6. Add the desired mixture amount, and spread in an even layer with a spoon.
7. Cook for about 2-3 minutes.
8. Carefully flip the side and cook for another minute.
9. Repeat with the remaining mixture.
10. Enjoy warm with the drizzling of maple syrup.

Banana Waffles

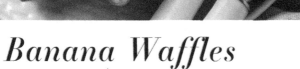

SERVES 5

Ingredients

- [ ] 2 tbsp. flaxseed meal
- [ ] 6 tbsp. warm water
- [ ] 2 bananas, peeled and mashed
- [ ] 1 C. creamy almond butter
- [ ] ¼ C. full-fat coconut milk
- [ ] pinch of nutmeg
- [ ] pinch of cinnamon

Directions

1. Blend the flaxseed meal and warm water in a small bowl with nutmeg and cinnamon. Set aside for 10 minutes.
2. Add the bananas, almond butter, and coconut milk and whisk to incorporate.
3. Preheat the waffle iron and lightly grease it with baking spray.
4. Place the desired amount of the mixture in the preheated waffle iron.
5. Cook for about 3-4 minutes.
6. Repeat with the remaining mixture.
7. Enjoy warm with your favorite topping.

Oats, Nuts & Seeds Muesli

SERVES 20

Ingredients

- [ ] 6 C. rolled oats
- [ ] 1 C. dried coconut, shredded
- [ ] 1 C. raw almonds, sliced
- [ ] ¾ C. flaxseed meal
- [ ] ½ C. raw pumpkin seeds
- [ ] ¼ C. raw sunflower seeds
- [ ] ¼ C. maple syrup
- [ ] 1 tbsp. olive oil
- [ ] 2 tbsp. water
- [ ] ½ C. dried fruit (cherries, apricots)

Directions

1. Preheat your oven to 300°F.
2. Mix all the ingredients except the dried fruit into a large bowl.
3. Spread the mixture onto a large baking tray and bake for about 20 minutes.
4. Take the baking tray from the oven and blend in the dried fruit.
5. Enjoy as oatmeal or overnight oats, topped with fresh fruit & maple syrup.

Eggless Tomato Omelet

SERVES 4

Ingredients

- [ ] 1 C. chickpea flour (or rice flour)
- [ ] ¼ tsp. ground turmeric
- [ ] ¼ tsp. red chili powder
- [ ] Pinch of salt
- [ ] 1½-2 C. water
- [ ] 1 medium onion, finely chopped
- [ ] 2 medium tomatoes, finely chopped
- [ ] 2 tbsp. fresh cilantro, chopped
- [ ] 2 tbsp. olive oil, divided

Directions

1. Mix the flour, spices, and salt in a large bowl.
2. Add the water and blend thoroughly.
3. Add the onion, tomatoes, and cilantro and gently blend to incorporate.
4. Heat ½ tbsp of oil over medium heat in a large non-stick frying pan.
5. Spread ½ of the batter to cover the pan.
6. Cook each side evenly for 2-3 minutes.
7. Repeat with the remaining mixture.

Tofu & Veggie Scramble

SERVES 2

Ingredients

- [ ] ½ tbsp. olive oil
- [ ] 1 small onion, finely chopped
- [ ] 1 green onion leaf
- [ ] 1 C. fresh kale, tough ribs removed and finely chopped
- [ ] 1 C. cherry tomatoes, finely chopped
- [ ] 1½ C. firm tofu, pressed, drained and crumbled
- [ ] Pinch of ground turmeric
- [ ] Salt and ground black pepper

Directions

1. Heat oil over medium heat in a wok and sauté the onion for about 4-5 minutes.
2. Add the kale and tomatoes and cook for about 1-2 minutes.
3. Add the tofu, turmeric, salt, and pepper and cook for 6-8 minutes.
4. Put chopped green onion on top.
5. Enjoy hot.

VEGGIES
Frittata

 PREP 15 MIN COOK 45 MIN  SERVES 8

Ingredients

- ☐ 1 (14-oz.) block firm tofu
- ☐ 2 tbsp. tapioca starch
- ☐ ¼ C. nutritional yeast
- ☐ 1 tsp. garlic powder
- ☐ ¼ tsp. ground turmeric
- ☐ ¼ C. unsweetened almond milk
- ☐ Non-stick baking spray
- ☐ 1 medium onion, chopped
- ☐ 4 oz. fresh mushrooms, sliced
- ☐ 1 bell pepper, seeded and chopped
- ☐ 3 C. fresh spinach, chopped
- ☐ Salt, as desired

Directions

1. For preheating, set your oven to 350°F.
2. Add tofu, tapioca flour, nutritional yeast, spices, and almond milk into a food processor and process to form a smooth mixture.
3. Lightly grease an ovenproof cast iron wok with baking spray and heat over medium heat.
4. Cook the onions and mushrooms for about 1-2 minutes.
5. Add bell pepper and spinach and cook for another 2-3 minutes.
6. Pour the tofu mixture and gently blend to incorporate.
7. Bake for about 40 minutes.
8. Take it out of the oven and let the frittata cool for 15 minutes.
9. Cut into serving portions and enjoy.

BROCCOLI
Quiche

 PREP 15 MIN COOK 60 MIN  SERVES 4

Ingredients

- [ ] 1 C. water
- [ ] Pinch of salt and pepper
- [ ] 1/3 C. bulgur wheat
- [ ] ¾ tbsp. light sesame oil
- [ ] 1½ C. fresh mushrooms, sliced
- [ ] 2 C. broccoli, chopped
- [ ] 1 onion, chopped
- [ ] 16 oz. Firm tofu drained and cubed
- [ ] ¾ tbsp. white miso
- [ ] 1¼ tbsp. tahini
- [ ] 1 tbsp. low-sodium soy sauce
- [ ] Fresh basil leaves for serving

Directions

1. Preheat your oven to 350°F. Lightly grease a pie dish with baking spray.
2. Add water and salt over medium heat into a pot and boil.
3. Blend in the bulgur and cook until boiling.
4. Turn the heat low and simmer, covered, for about 12-15 minutes.
5. Place the cooked bulgur in the pie dish and press it into the bottom with a spoon.
6. Bake for about 12 minutes.
7. Take off from the oven and set aside to cool.
8. Heat oil in a wok and cook the mushrooms, broccoli, and onion for 10 minutes.
9. In a food processor, add the remaining ingredients and process.
10. Transfer the tofu mixture into the bowl with the veggie mixture & blend thoroughly.
11. Place the veggie mixture over the crust evenly.
12. Bake for about 30 minutes.
13. Take it out from the oven and set the pie dish aside for at least 10 minutes. Enjoy.

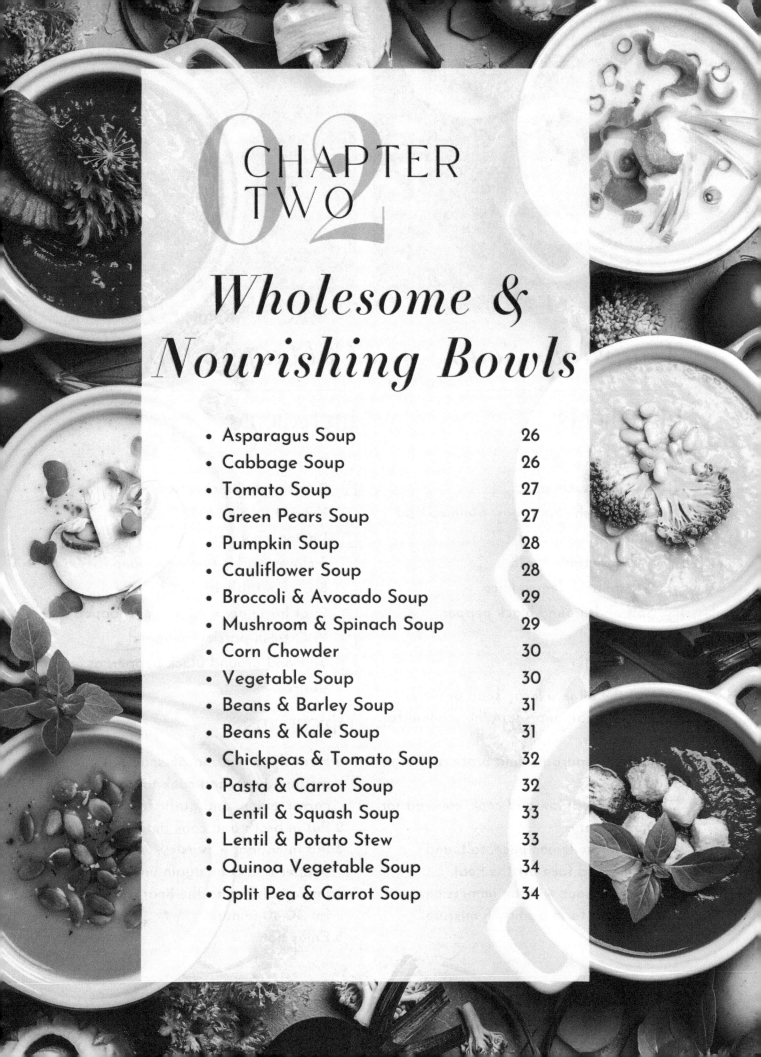

02

CHAPTER TWO

Wholesome & Nourishing Bowls

Asparagus Soup

SERVES 4

Ingredients

- ☐ 1 tbsp. olive oil
- ☐ 3 scallions, chopped
- ☐ 1½ lb. fresh asparagus, trimmed and chopped
- ☐ 4 C. vegetable broth
- ☐ 2 tbsp. fresh lemon juice
- ☐ Salt and ground black pepper

Directions

1. Heat the oil in a large soup pot over medium heat, and sauté the scallion for 4-5 minutes.
2. Blend in asparagus and broth and cook until boiling.
3. Turn the heat low and cook, covered for 25-30 minutes.
4. Blend in the lemon juice, salt, and pepper, and take off the heat.
5. Blend the soup with an immersion blender to form a smooth mixture.
6. Enjoy hot.

Cabbage Soup

SERVES 8

Ingredients

- ☐ 2 tbsp. olive oil
- ☐ 2 celery stalks, chopped
- ☐ 1 carrot, peeled and chopped
- ☐ 1 onion, chopped
- ☐ 3 cloves garlic, finely chopped
- ☐ 8 C. vegetable broth
- ☐ ½ of large head cabbage, chopped
- ☐ ½ C. fresh parsley, chopped
- ☐ Salt and ground black pepper, as desired

Directions

1. Heat the oil in a large soup pot over medium heat, and cook the celery, carrot, onion, and garlic for 4-5 minutes.
2. Put in broth and cook until boiling.
3. Put in cabbage, parsley, salt, and pepper and cook again until boiling.
4. Immediately turn the heat low and cook for 30-40 minutes.
5. Enjoy hot.

Tomato Soup

SERVES 4

Ingredients

- [ ] 2 tbsp. coconut oil
- [ ] 2 carrots, peeled and chopped
- [ ] 1 large onion, chopped
- [ ] 3 cloves garlic, minced
- [ ] 5 large tomatoes, chopped
- [ ] ¼ C. fresh basil, chopped
- [ ] 1 tbsp. tomato paste
- [ ] 3 C. vegetable broth
- [ ] ¼ C. unsweetened coconut milk
- [ ] Salt and ground black pepper

Directions

1. Melt coconut oil in a large soup pot over medium heat, and cook the carrots and onion for about 10 minutes.
2. Add in garlic and cook for 2 minutes.
3. Blend in tomatoes, basil, tomato paste, and broth, and cook until boiling.
4. Turn the heat to low & cook for 30 min.
5. Blend in the coconut milk, salt, and pepper, and set it aside for 10 minutes.
6. Blend the soup with an immersion blender to form a smooth mixture. Enjoy.

Green Peas Soup

SERVES 5

Ingredients

- [ ] 2 tbsp. refined olive oil
- [ ] ½ of onion, chopped
- [ ] 3 cloves garlic, sliced
- [ ] 5 C. frozen green peas
- [ ] 1/3 C. fresh parsley, chopped
- [ ] 4 C. vegetable broth
- [ ] 1 (13½-oz.) can light coconut milk
- [ ] Salt and ground black pepper, as desired

Directions

1. Heat oil in a large pot over medium heat, and cook the onion and garlic for 4-5 minutes.
2. Put in peas, parsley, broth, coconut milk, salt, and pepper, and cook until boiling.
3. Immediately turn the heat to low and cook with the cover for 8-10 minutes.
4. Remove the soup pot from the heat and blend the soup with an immersion blender to form a smooth mixture.
5. Enjoy immediately.

Pumpkin Soup

SERVES 4

Ingredients

- [ ] 2 tsp. olive oil
- [ ] 1 onion, chopped
- [ ] 1 tsp. fresh ginger, chopped
- [ ] 2 cloves garlic, chopped
- [ ] 2 tbsp. fresh cilantro, chopped
- [ ] 3 C. pumpkin, peeled and cubed
- [ ] 4¼ C. vegetable broth
- [ ] Salt and ground black pepper, as desired

Directions

1. Heat oil over medium heat in a large soup pot and sauté the onion, ginger, garlic, and cilantro for around 4-5 minutes.
2. Add the pumpkin and broth and cook until boiling
3. Turn the heat to low and simmer, covered for around 15 minutes.
4. Remove from the heat, and with an immersion blender, blend the soup to form a smooth mixture.
5. Enjoy hot.

Cauliflower Soup

SERVES 4

Ingredients

- [ ] 2 tbsp. olive oil
- [ ] 1 large onion, chopped
- [ ] 2 carrots, peeled and chopped
- [ ] 2 cloves garlic, minced
- [ ] 1 tsp. ground cumin
- [ ] ¼ tsp. red pepper flakes
- [ ] 1 head cauliflower, chopped
- [ ] 4½ C. vegetable broth
- [ ] Salt and ground black pepper, as desired

Directions

1. Heat the oil over medium heat in a large pot and sauté the onion and carrot for around 5-6 minutes.
2. Add the garlic and spices and sauté for around 1 minute.
3. Add the cauliflower and broth and cook until boiling.
4. Turn the heat to low and simmer for around 15 minutes.
5. Blend in salt and pepper and enjoy hot.

Broccoli & Avocado Soup

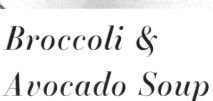 SERVES 4

Ingredients

- ☐ 2 tbsp. olive oil
- ☐ ½ C. onion, chopped
- ☐ 1 clove garlic, minced
- ☐ 1 tbsp. fresh thyme, chopped
- ☐ 4 C. broccoli florets
- ☐ 4 C. vegetable broth
- ☐ 1 avocado, peeled, pitted and chopped

Directions

1. Heat the oil in a large soup pot over medium heat and sauté the onion.
2. Add garlic and thyme and sauté for another minute.
3. Add broccoli and cook for about 3 min.
4. Blend in the broth and cook until boiling over high heat.
5. Turn the heat to medium-low and cook with the cover for 30-35 minutes.
6. Turn off the heat and add avocado.
7. Blend the soup with an immersion blender to form a smooth mixture. Enjoy.

Mushroom & Spinach Soup

SERVES 4

Ingredients

- ☐ 1 tsp. olive oil
- ☐ 1 small onion, finely chopped
- ☐ 4 cloves garlic, finely chopped
- ☐ ½ lb. fresh mushrooms, chopped
- ☐ 1 C. fresh spinach, roughly chopped
- ☐ Salt and ground black pepper
- ☐ 2 C. coconut cream
- ☐ 2 C. vegetable broth

Directions

1. Heat oil in a soup pot over medium heat, and cook the onion and garlic for 4-5 minutes.
2. Put mushrooms in and sauté until lightly browned, 3-4 minutes.
3. Add spinach, salt, and pepper and cook with the cover for 3-5 minutes.
4. Blend in water and coconut cream and take off the heat.
5. Enjoy hot.
6. Serve with bread if desired.

Corn Chowder

SERVES 4

Ingredients

- [ ] 2 tbsp. olive oil
- [ ] 2 celery stalks, chopped
- [ ] 4 scallions, chopped, green tops reserved
- [ ] 2 cloves garlic, minced
- [ ] 3 medium potatoes, peeled & chopped
- [ ] 1 red bell pepper, chopped
- [ ] 1 bay leaf
- [ ] Salt and ground black pepper
- [ ] 3 C. vegetable broth
- [ ] 3 C. fresh corn kernels
- [ ] 1 C. coconut cream

Directions

1. Heat oil over medium heat in a large soup pot and sauté celery, scallion bulbs, bell pepper, and garlic for 7-8 minutes.
2. Add potatoes, corn, bay leaf, salt, pepper, and broth, and simmer for 15 minutes.
3. Remove a bay leaf. Blend half the soup with coconut cream in a food processor, then return it to the pot. Simmer for 5 more min. Stir in scallion greens. Enjoy.

Vegetable Soup

SERVES 8

Ingredients

- [ ] 1½ tbsp. olive oil
- [ ] 4 medium carrots, peeled & chopped
- [ ] 1 medium onion, chopped
- [ ] 2 celery stalks, chopped
- [ ] 2 C. fresh tomatoes, finely chopped
- [ ] 3½ C. small cauliflower florets
- [ ] 3½ C. small broccoli florets
- [ ] 8 C. vegetable broth
- [ ] 3 tbsp. fresh lemon juice
- [ ] Salt, as desired
- [ ] Dill and Parsley for garnish

Directions

1. Heat oil over medium heat in a large soup pot and sauté the carrots, celery, and onion for 7-8 minutes.
2. Add the tomatoes and cook for 2-3 min.
3. Add the vegetables and broth and cook until boiling over high heat.
4. Turn the heat to low and cook with the cover for about 30-35 minutes.
5. Blend in lemon juice and salt.
6. Garnish with dill and parsley. Enjoy.

30

Beans & Barley Soup

SERVES 4

Ingredients

- [ ] 1 tbsp. olive oil
- [ ] 1 white onion, chopped
- [ ] 2 celery stalks, chopped
- [ ] 1 large carrot, peeled and chopped
- [ ] 2 tbsp. fresh rosemary, chopped
- [ ] 2 cloves garlic, minced
- [ ] 2 C. tomatoes, chopped
- [ ] 4 C. vegetable broth
- [ ] 1 C. pearl barley
- [ ] 2 C. canned white beans

Directions

1. Heat oil over medium heat in a large soup pot and sauté the onion, celery, and carrot for 4-5 minutes.
2. Add the tomatoes, garlic, and rosemary and cook for 4-5 minutes.
3. Add barley and broth and simmer, covered, for about 30 minutes.
4. Blend in beans and simmer for 5 min.
5. Garnish with parsley and enjoy hot.

Beans & Kale Soup

SERVES 2

Ingredients

- [ ] 1 tbsp. olive oil
- [ ] 1 small onion, chopped
- [ ] 1 small tomato, chopped
- [ ] 2 C. vegetable broth
- [ ] 3 C. fresh kale, tough ribs removed and chopped
- [ ] 1 C. canned white beans, drained
- [ ] Salt and ground black pepper, as desired

Directions

1. Heat oil in a medium soup pot over medium-high heat and cook the onion for about 5 minutes.
2. Put in tomato and broth and cook until boiling.
3. Put in kale and beans and cook for another 5-6 minutes.
4. Add salt and pepper.
5. Enjoy hot.

Chickpeas & Tomato Soup

SERVES 4

Ingredients

- [ ] 1 tbsp. olive oil
- [ ] 1 medium onion, chopped
- [ ] 2 C. carrots, peeled and chopped
- [ ] 2 cloves garlic, minced
- [ ] 1 15 oz can crushed tomatoes
- [ ] 2 C. vegetable broth
- [ ] 2 15 oz cans of chickpeas
- [ ] 1 C. fresh spinach, chopped
- [ ] 1 tbsp. fresh lemon juice

Directions

1. Heat oil over medium heat in a large pot and sauté the onion, carrot, and garlic for 6-7 minutes.
2. Add the tomatoes and cook for 2-3 min.
3. Add the broth and cook until boiling.
4. Turn the heat to low and simmer for 10 minutes. Then add in the chickpeas and spinach and simmer for about 5 minutes.
5. Add lemon juice, salt, pepper, and garnish with parsley. Enjoy hot.

Pasta & Carrot Soup

SERVES 4

Ingredients

- [ ] 2 tbsp. olive oil
- [ ] 1 C. celery, sliced
- [ ] 1 small carrot, peeled and sliced
- [ ] 1 onion, chopped
- [ ] 1 clove garlic, smashed
- [ ] ½ C. vegan pasta
- [ ] 4 C. vegetable broth
- [ ] 2 tbsp. fresh parsley and dill, chopped
- [ ] 1 bell pepper, chopped
- [ ] 1 tbsp. fresh lemon juice

Directions

1. Heat oil over medium heat in a large soup pot. Add celery, carrot, onion, bell pepper, and garlic and cook for 8 min.
2. Add in broth and pasta and cook until boiling.
3. Immediately cover the soup pot and cook for about 8-10 minutes.
4. Blend in parsley, lemon juice, salt, and pepper, and enjoy.

Lentil & Squash Soup

SERVES 8

Ingredients

- ☐ 2 tbsp. olive oil
- ☐ ½ C. carrot, peeled and chopped
- ☐ ¼ C. celery, finely chopped
- ☐ ¼ C. onion, chopped
- ☐ 2 tsp. garlic, finely chopped
- ☐ 1 medium tomato, chopped
- ☐ 1 tsp. dried basil
- ☐ 8 C. water
- ☐ ½ C. split lentils, soaked and drained
- ☐ 3 C. butternut squash, peeled & cubed
- ☐ 2 tbsp. fresh rosemary, chopped

Directions

1. Heat oil in a soup pot over medium-low heat, and cook the carrot, celery, onion, and garlic for about 5 minutes.
2. Blend in tomato, basil, lentils, squash, and water and cook until boiling.
3. Immediately turn the heat to low and cook with the cover for 40-45 minutes.
4. Add salt & pepper, garnish with rosemary.

Lentil & Potato Stew

SERVES 6

Ingredients

- ☐ 2 tbsp. olive oil
- ☐ 2 carrots, peeled and chopped
- ☐ 2 potatoes, peeled and chopped
- ☐ 1 yellow onion, chopped
- ☐ 3 garlic cloves, chopped
- ☐ 2 C. red lentils, rinsed
- ☐ 1 (15-oz.) can diced tomatoes with juice
- ☐ 8 C. vegetable broth
- ☐ 1 tsp. dried oregano
- ☐ Fresh parsley leaves

Directions

1. Heat oil in a large soup pot over medium heat. Add the carrots, potato, onion, and garlic and cook for 4-5 min.
2. Blend in lentils, tomatoes, broth, and paprika, and cook until boiling.
3. Immediately turn the heat low and cook for 30-40 minutes.
4. Add salt and pepper, garnish with parsley and enjoy hot.

Quinoa Vegetable Soup

SERVES 6

Ingredients

- [ ] 2 tbsp. olive oil
- [ ] 1 onion, cut up
- [ ] 4 cloves garlic, cut up
- [ ] ½ tsp oregano, salt and black pepper
- [ ] 1½ cups quinoa, rinsed
- [ ] 4 tomatoes, cut up
- [ ] 1 bell pepper, seeded and cut up
- [ ] 3 celery stalks, cut up
- [ ] ¾ cup fresh basil, cut up
- [ ] 6 cups water
- [ ] 1 medium carrot, peeled and cut up

Directions

1. Heat oil in a soup pot over medium-low heat, and cook the carrot, celery, onion, bell pepper, and garlic for 7 minutes.
2. Add water, quinoa, tomatoes, and basil, and cook until boiling.
3. Immediately turn the heat to low and cook with the cover for 20 minutes.
4. Add salt, pepper, and oregano. Enjoy.

Split Pea & Carrot Soup

SERVES 6

Ingredients

- [ ] 1 tbsp. olive oil
- [ ] 1 C. carrot, peeled and chopped
- [ ] 1 C. onion, peeled and chopped
- [ ] 2 cloves garlic, peeled and minced
- [ ] 2 C. dry split peas, rinsed
- [ ] 3 fresh sprigs of rosemary
- [ ] 1 bay leaf
- [ ] 6 C. vegetable broth

Directions

1. Heat the oil over medium heat in a large pot and sauté the carrots, onions, and garlic for about 5 minutes.
2. Add the remaining ingredients except rosemary and bring them to a boil.
3. Turn the heat to low and simmer, partially covered, for about 30 minutes.
4. Discard bay leaf and blend half of the soup with an immersion blender to form a smooth mixture, then pour back.
5. Garnish with rosemary and enjoy.

03
CHAPTER THREE

Fiesta Combos

CAULIFLOWER
Lettuce Wraps

 PREP 15 MIN  COOK 20 MIN   SERVES 6

- ☐ 1 large cauliflower head, cut into florets
- ☐ 2 tbsp. olive oil
- ☐ 2 tbsp. fresh lime juice
- ☐ Salt and ground black pepper, as desired
- ☐ 12 large lettuce leaves
- ☐ 2 C. purple cabbage, thinly sliced
- ☐ 2 C. cherry tomatoes, sliced
- ☐ 3 tbsp. walnuts, chopped
- ☐ 2 tbsp. parsley, chopped
- ☐ 1 C. Cilantro & Avocado Dressing

1. Preheat your oven to 425°F. Line a baking tray with baking paper.
2. In a large bowl, blend cauliflower, oil, lime juice, salt, and pepper, tossing to incorporate.
3. Place the cauliflower on the baking tray.
4. Bake for about 15-20 minutes.
5. Take it out of the oven and set it aside to cool.
6. Arrange the lettuce leaves on serving plates.
7. Divide the cauliflower, cabbage, and tomato onto each lettuce leaf.
8. Sprinkle with walnuts and parsley.
9. Pour the dressing over each wrap and serve.
10. Enjoy immediately.

Directions

Spicy Black Bean Tortillas

SERVES 4

Ingredients

- [ ] 2 tbsp. olive oil
- [ ] 1 14-ounce can of black beans (rinsed and drained)
- [ ] 1 jalapeno (small dice), seeds removed
- [ ] 2 cloves garlic, minced
- [ ] 2 medium tomatoes (small dice)
- [ ] ½ medium sweet onion (small dice)
- [ ] ½ red bell pepper chopped
- [ ] 4 tbsp. guacamole
- [ ] 2 tbsp. fresh lime juice
- [ ] 4 tortillas
- [ ] 4 lettuce leaves

Directions

1. In a large wok, heat oil over medium heat. Add beans, tomato, pepper, garlic, salt, jalapeno and saute for 6-8 minutes.
2. Arrange the tortilla onto serving plates.
3. Put lettuce leaves on each tortilla, then top with beans and guacamole, and sprinkle with lime juice. Serve.

Veggie Lettuce Wraps

SERVES 3

Ingredients

- [ ] 1 C. multi-colored bell peppers, seeded and julienned
- [ ] 1 C. carrots, peeled and sliced
- [ ] ¼ C. fresh chives
- [ ] Salt, as desired
- [ ] 6 large lettuce leaves
- [ ] 3 small tomatoes, sliced
- [ ] 3 soft vegan plant-powered tortillas

Directions

1. Combine the bell peppers, carrots, chives, tomatoes, and salt in a large bowl and blend thoroughly.
2. Arrange the tortillas and lettuce leaves on a serving platter.
3. Divide the veggie mixture onto each lettuce leaf.
4. Add protein: make your wrap more filling by adding chickpeas, black beans, or a scoop of quinoa.
5. Enjoy immediately.

Tofu & Veggie Lettuce Wraps

SERVES 5

Ingredients

- ☐ 1 tbsp. olive oil
- ☐ 14 oz. extra-firm tofu pressed, drained, and cut into cubes
- ☐ 1 tsp. curry powder
- ☐ Salt and ground pepper, as desired
- ☐ 5 lettuce leaves
- ☐ 1 small carrot, peeled and julienned
- ☐ 1 C. champions, sliced
- ☐ 2 tbsp. fresh cilantro, chopped
- ☐ Marinara or Balsamic Vinaigrette sauce

Directions

1. Heat oil in a wok over medium heat. Add tofu, champions, curry powder, salt and pepper, and cook for 5-6 minutes, stirring frequently.
2. Take off from the heat and set aside to cool slightly.
3. Arrange lettuce leaves on a serving plate.
4. Divide tofu and carrot over each leaf.
5. Garnish with cilantro and add sauce.

Avocado & Veggie Tortilla Wraps

SERVES 2

Ingredients

- ☐ 2 vegan tortillas, warmed
- ☐ ¼ C. hummus
- ☐ 1 red onion, thinly sliced
- ☐ ½ of avocado peeled, pitted & sliced
- ☐ ½ of medium red bell pepper, seeded and thinly sliced
- ☐ ½ C. lettuce, torn
- ☐ 1 big tomato, sliced
- ☐ 2 parsley leaves

Directions

1. Arrange the tortillas onto a smooth surface.
2. Place the hummus evenly onto the center of each wrap and top it with avocado and vegetables.
3. Carefully fold the edges of each tortilla over the filling to roll up.
4. Cut each roll in half crosswise and garnish with parsley.
5. Enjoy.

Chocolate Banana Toast

SERVES 1

Ingredients

- [ ] 2 vegan bread slices
- [ ] 1 tbsp. dark chocolate
- [ ] 1 banana, peeled and sliced
- [ ] ½ tsp. ground cinnamon
- [ ] ½ tsp. nutmeg
- [ ] 1 tbsp. agave syrup
- [ ] 2 tbsp. coconut yogurt
- [ ] 1 tbsp seeds (sunflower, pumpkin)

Directions

1. Toast the bread slices.
2. Melt chocolate and spread it on one side of each bread slice.
3. Mix yogurt with agave syrup and spread it on each bread slice.
4. Place banana slices over the bread and sprinkle with cinnamon and nutmeg.
5. Add seeds on top and enjoy.

Avocado & Tomato Toast

SERVES 4

Ingredients

- [ ] 1 avocado, peeled, pitted and sliced
- [ ] 1 large tomato, sliced
- [ ] ½ C. green olives
- [ ] ½ C. basil leaves
- [ ] 4 vegan bread slices toasted
- [ ] Plant butter

Directions

1. Toast the bread slices and arrange them on a plate.
2. Spread butter over each slice.
3. Place avocado, tomatoes, and olives.
4. Garnish with basil leaves.
5. Cut the bread diagonally and enjoy.

Veggies Sandwich

 SERVES 4

Ingredients

- ☐ 1 large cucumber, sliced
- ☐ 1 large tomato, sliced
- ☐ ½ C. red onion, thinly sliced
- ☐ 1 C. lettuce leaves, torn
- ☐ ¼ tbsp. fresh lemon juice
- ☐ ¼ tsp. ground cumin
- ☐ Salt and ground black pepper
- ☐ 1 avocado, sliced and mashed
- ☐ ½ C. hummus
- ☐ 8 vegan bread slices, toasted
- ☐ 4 pinches of microgreens

Directions

1. Blend cucumber, tomato, onion, lettuce, lemon juice, and spices in a large bowl.
2. Spread hummus over 4 slices of bread.
3. Divide tomato, cucumber, onion, and lettuce over 4 slices. Top with microgreens and avocado.
4. Cover with remaining slices.
5. Enjoy.

Chickpeas Sandwich

 SERVES 4

Ingredients

- ☐ 1 (15½-oz.) cans of chickpeas, drained
- ☐ 4 tbsp. vegan mayonnaise
- ☐ 3 tbsp. fresh lemon juice
- ☐ 2 tsp. Dijon mustard
- ☐ Salt and ground black pepper, as desired
- ☐ 8 vegan bread slices, toasted
- ☐ 4 green lettuce leaves, torn
- ☐ 2 scallions, chopped
- ☐ 1 big tomato, sliced

Directions

1. Mash chickpeas, 2 tbsp. of mayonnaise, lemon juice, mustard, salt, and pepper in a large stone pestle with mortar.
2. Spread the mixture on one side of each of the 4 bread slices, and the other 4 bread slices with the rest of the mayonnaise.
3. Place lettuce, onion, tomato.
4. Cover with remaining slices and enjoy.

Mixed Fruit Salad

SERVES 10

Ingredients

- [ ] 2 C. kiwi fruit, peeled and sliced
- [ ] 2 C. apple, cut into chunks
- [ ] 2 C. fresh raspberries
- [ ] 2 C. fresh blackberries
- [ ] 2 C. fresh blueberries
- [ ] 1 C. fresh grapes
- [ ] 2 C. mandarines, cut into chunks
- [ ] ¼ C. maple syrup
- [ ] 2-3 tbsp. fresh lime juice

Directions

1. Add all fruits and berries, maple syrup, and lime juice into a large salad bowl and toss to incorporate.
2. Set aside for about 15 minutes.
3. Put into serving bowls and enjoy.

Apple & Walnut Salad

SERVES 6

Ingredients

- [ ] 3 large apples, cored and sliced
- [ ] 4 C. fresh kale, tough ribs removed and chopped
- [ ] ¼ C. pecans or walnuts
- [ ] 1 C. pomegranate seeds
- [ ] 3 tbsp. olive oil
- [ ] 2 tbsp. balsamic vinegar dressing
- [ ] 2 tbsp. maple syrup
- [ ] ¼ tsp. garlic powder

Directions

1. In a large salad bowl, add the kale, pomegranate seeds, apple slices, and nuts.
2. In a glass jar, add all of the salad dressing ingredients and whisk until combined.
3. Drizzle the dressing over top of the salad.
4. Enjoy immediately.

Mango & Avocado Salad

SERVES 4

Ingredients

- [ ] 4 mango, peeled, pitted and cubed
- [ ] 4 avocado, peeled, pitted and cubed
- [ ] 1 C. cherry tomatoes, cut
- [ ] 1 C. cucumber, cubed
- [ ] 1 C. fresh cilantro, chopped
- [ ] 4 tbsp. small diced red onion
- [ ] 4 tbsp. extra-virgin olive oil
- [ ] 4 tbsp. fresh lime juice
- [ ] 4 tbsp. maple syrup
- [ ] 1 tsp. cumin
- [ ] ½ tsp. chili powder
- [ ] 1 tsp. salt and ground black pepper

Directions

1. In a large serving bowl, whisk together the olive oil, lime juice, honey, cumin, chili powder, salt, and pepper until well combined and emulsified.
2. Add the mango, avocado, tomatoes, cucumber, onions, and cilantro on top and toss to combine them evenly. Serve.

Cucumber & Tomato Salad

SERVES 4

Ingredients

- [ ] 1 cucumber, thinly cut
- [ ] 2 C. halved cherry tomatoes
- [ ] 2 C. romano salad leaves, torn
- [ ] 5 oz. Vegan Feta cheese, cubed small
- [ ] ⅓ C. thinly sliced red onion
- [ ] ⅓ C. pitted black or Kalamata olives
- [ ] ¼ C. extra-virgin olive oil
- [ ] 3 tbsp. red wine vinegar
- [ ] 1 garlic clove, minced
- [ ] 1 sprinkle of dried oregano
- [ ] ¼ tsp. Dijon mustard
- [ ] ½ tsp. salt and ground black pepper

Directions

1. In a small bowl, whisk together olive oil, vinegar, garlic, mustard, salt, & pepper.
2. Arrange the cucumber, cherry tomatoes, feta cheese, red onions, and olives on a large platter. Drizzle with the dressing and very gently toss. Sprinkle with oregano and serve.

CAESAR
Salad

 PREP 15 MIN  COOK 12 MIN  SERVES 6

Ingredients

For the Croutons:

☐ 2 C. vegan bread cubes

☐ 2 tbsp. olive oil

☐ 2 cloves garlic, minced

For the Salad:

☐ 2 romaine lettuce heads, chopped

☐ ½ C. vegan parmesan cheese, shredded

For the Vegan Cashew Dressing:

☐ 3 tsp fresh lemon juice

☐ 1 C. raw cashews

☐ ¾ C. water

☐ 2 cloves garlic, minced

☐ 1 tbsp. Dijon mustard

☐ 1 tbsp. capers drained

☐ 1 tbsp. vegan Worcestershire sauce

☐ salt, as desired

Directions

1. For preheating, set your oven to 350°F.
2. Add bread cubes, oil, and garlic to a bowl for croutons and toss to incorporate.
3. Spread the bread cubes onto a baking tray.
4. Bake for 10-12 minutes, then take them out to cool.
5. Soak the cashews in a bowl of hot water for about 5 minutes for the dressing.
6. Drain the cashews and transfer them into a blender.
7. Add the remaining ingredients and process to form a smooth mixture.
8. In a large salad bowl, add lettuce, croutons, and dressing and toss to incorporate.
9. Sprinkle with parmesan and enjoy.

43

Beans & Corn Salad

SERVES 6

Ingredients

- ☐ 3 tbsp. olive oil
- ☐ 2½ tbsp. fresh lime juice
- ☐ 1 tsp. date maple syrup
- ☐ 1 clove garlic, finely chopped
- ☐ ¼ tsp. red chili powder
- ☐ 1 (14½-oz.) can black beans, drained
- ☐ 1 C. frozen corn, thawed
- ☐ 1 C. tomato, chopped
- ☐ 1 C. bell pepper, seeded and chopped
- ☐ 1 /3 C. red onion, chopped
- ☐ 1 cucumber, chopped
- ☐ ½ C. fresh parsley, chopped

Directions

1. For the dressing, add oil, lime juice, maple syrup, garlic, red chili powder, salt, and pepper to a small bowl and whisk to incorporate.
2. Place all salad ingredients into a large salad bowl and mix. Place the dressing over the salad and toss to incorporate.

Chickpeas & Veggie Salad

SERVES 4

Ingredients

- ☐ 3 C. cooked chickpeas
- ☐ 2 C., cucumber, chopped
- ☐ 1 C. cherry tomatoes, halved
- ☐ 1 C. radishes, trimmed and sliced
- ☐ 6 C. fresh baby arugula
- ☐ 4 tbsp. scallion, chopped
- ☐ 4 tbsp. fresh parsley leaves, chopped
- ☐ 1 tsp. sesame seeds
- ☐ **For the Dressing:**
- ☐ 1 clove garlic, finely chopped
- ☐ 3 tbsp. olive oil
- ☐ 1 tbsp. balsamic vinegar
- ☐ 1 tbsp. fresh lemon juice

Directions

1. For the salad, add all ingredients, salt, pepper into a large serving bowl & mix.
2. For the dressing, add all ingredients to another bowl and whisk to incorporate.
3. Pour dressing over salad & lightly blend.
4. Sprinkle with sesame seeds. Enjoy.

Pasta & Veggie Salad

 SERVES 6

Ingredients

- ☐ 12 oz. plant-based Fusilli pasta
- ☐ 2 C. cherry tomatoes, halved
- ☐ 1 C. cucumber, thinly sliced
- ☐ 1 C. broccoli, chopped
- ☐ ½ C. black olives, sliced
- ☐ 3 tbsp. canned corn
- **For the Vinaigrette:**
- ☐ 2 tbsp. balsamic vinegar
- ☐ 2 tbsp. olive oil
- ☐ 1 tbsp. fresh lemon juice
- ☐ 1 tsp. sesame oil

Directions

1. Add pasta to a pot of salted boiling water and cook for about 8-10 minutes.
2. Drain pasta and transfer it into a bowl.
3. Add the remaining salad ingredients to the pasta bowl and gently mix.
4. For the vinaigrette, in a small bowl, add all the ingredients & whisk to incorporate.
5. Pour the vinaigrette over the salad and gently blend to incorporate. Enjoy.

Pomegranate & Couscous Salad

 SERVES 6

Ingredients

- ☐ 4 C. couscous
- ☐ 5 C. boiling water
- ☐ 1 C. pomegranate arils
- ☐ 2 cucumber, chopped
- ☐ ½ C. fresh mint leaves
- ☐ 4 tbsp. olive oil
- ☐ 6 tbsp. fresh lemon juice
- ☐ 2 tbsp. lemon zest
- ☐ 2 tbsp. agave syrup

Directions

1. Add the couscous to boiling water with 2 tbsp. of lemon juice into a large heatproof bowl and cover the bowl.
2. Set aside for 5 minutes.
3. With a fork, fluff the lemon couscous.
4. In a small bowl, whisk the maple syrup, lemon juice, olive oil, and salt.
5. Add the couscous and remaining ingredients to a large serving bowl.
6. Pour the dressing over the top & toss well to coat. Serve with lemon wedges.

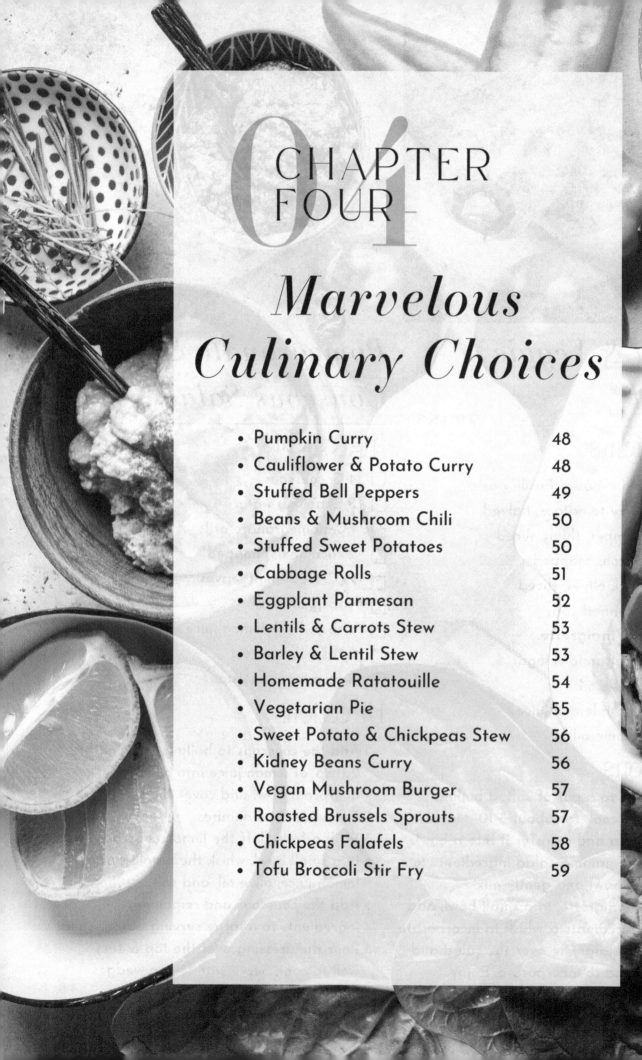

CHAPTER FOUR

04

Marvelous Culinary Choices

Pumpkin Curry

SERVES 4

Ingredients

- [ ] 2 tsp. olive oil
- [ ] 1 onion, chopped
- [ ] 1 tbsp. fresh ginger, minced
- [ ] 1 tbsp. garlic, minced
- [ ] 1 medium pumpkin, peeled and cubed
- [ ] 1 C. carrot, chopped
- [ ] 1 C. unsweetened coconut milk
- [ ] 2 C. vegetable broth
- [ ] 1 C. passata or tomato sauce
- [ ] 1 tbsp. curry powder
- [ ] 2 tsp. ground turmeric
- [ ] 2-3 tsp. salt and ground black pepper
- [ ] Fresh cilantro and scallion to garnish
- [ ] Cooked rice to serve

Directions

1. Heat oil over medium-high heat in a large pot. Add the onion, carrot, ginger, and garlic and cook for 4-5 minutes.
2. Add pumpkin, coconut milk, broth, and all spices, and cook until boiling.
3. Turn the heat to low and simmer for 20-25 min. Serve with rice. Garnish. Enjoy.

Cauliflower & Potato Curry

SERVES 2

Ingredients

- [ ] 2 tbsp. olive oil
- [ ] 3 cloves garlic, minced
- [ ] ½ tbsp. fresh ginger, minced
- [ ] 2 tsp. curry powder
- [ ] 4 medium tomatoes, finely chopped
- [ ] 2 potatoes, peeled and cubed
- [ ] 2 C. cauliflower, chopped
- [ ] 1 C. fresh green peas, shelled
- [ ] Salt and ground black pepper
- [ ] 1½ C. water
- [ ] Chapatis or vegan bread to serve

Directions

1. Heat the oil over medium heat in a large wok and sauté the garlic, ginger, and curry powder for 1 minute.
2. Add tomatoes, potatoes, and cauliflower, and cook for 3-5 minutes.
3. Add warm water and cook until boiling.
4. Turn the heat to medium-low and cook, covered for about 12-15 minutes.
5. Enjoy hot. Serve with Chapatis.

STUFFED
Bell Peppers

 PREP 15 MIN   COOK 35 MIN  SERVES 4

Ingredients

- [ ] ¾ C. uncooked couscous
- [ ] ¾ C. vegetable broth
- 4 bell peppers, tops removed
- [ ] 1 bell pepper, cubed
- [ ] 1 zucchini, peeled and cubed
- [ ] 1 C. plum tomatoes, chopped
- [ ] 1 small yellow onion, chopped
- [ ] 2 large cloves garlic, minced
- [ ] Salt and black pepper to taste
- [ ] 1 tsp. dried oregano
- [ ] 1 tbsp. olive oil
- [ ] 1 tbsp. fresh lemon juice

Directions

1. In a medium saucepan, bring the broth to a boil. Add the couscous, 1 tsp. of olive oil, salt, and stir. Cover, remove from the heat, and let stand for 10 minutes.
2. With a fork, fluff the couscous and let it cool completely.
3. Heat the oil over medium heat in a wok and sauté the garlic, zucchini, chopped bell pepper, and onion for 5 minutes.
4. Add the tomatoes and cook for another 3 minutes.
5. Add couscous and species and mix thoroughly.
6. For preheating, set your oven to 350°F. Line a baking sheet with baking paper.
7. Arrange bell peppers on a baking sheet.
8. Stuff bell peppers with couscous mixture and cover with their seeded covers.
9. Bake for about 35 minutes.
10. Garnish with basil and sprinkle with lemon juice.
11. Enjoy warm.

Beans & Mushroom Chili

SERVES 4

Ingredients

- [ ] 2 tbsp. avocado oil
- [ ] 1 medium onion, chopped
- [ ] 1 bell pepper, seeded and chopped
- [ ] 1 lb. fresh mushrooms, sliced
- [ ] 2 cloves garlic, minced
- [ ] 2 tsp. dried oregano
- [ ] 1 tbsp. red chili powder
- [ ] Salt and ground black pepper
- [ ] 8 oz. canned red kidney beans, drained
- [ ] 8 oz. canned white beans, drained
- [ ] 2 C. tomatoes, finely chopped
- [ ] 1½ C. vegetable broth

Directions

1. Heat oil over medium-low heat in a large Dutch oven, and cook the onions and bell pepper for about 8 minutes.
2. Add mushrooms, garlic, oregano, red chili, salt, and pepper, and cook for 6 minutes.
3. Blend in beans, tomatoes, and broth and cook until boiling. Turn the heat to low & simmer, covered for 25 minutes. Enjoy.

Stuffed Sweet Potatoes

SERVES 2

Ingredients

- [ ] 1 large sweet potato, halved
- [ ] ½ tbsp. olive oil, divided
- [ ] 1/3 C. canned chickpeas, drained
- [ ] 1/3 C. cooked quinoa
- [ ] Salt and ground black pepper to taste
- [ ] 2 tbsp. parsley, chopped
- [ ] ½ C. garlic lemon vegan yogurt

Directions

1. For preheating, set your oven to 375°F.
2. Rub sweet potato halves with olive oil and arrange them on a baking sheet cut side down.
3. Bake for 40 minutes.
4. In a bowl, blend chickpeas, quinoa, salt and pepper.
5. Stuff potato halves with the chickpea mixture and bake for 10 minutes.
6. Garnish with parsley.
7. For the sauce, stir together the yogurt, olive oil, lemon juice, garlic, and salt.
8. Enjoy immediately.

CABBAGE
Rolls

 PREP 20 MIN COOK 25 MIN SERVES 4

Ingredients

For the Filling:

- ☐ 1½ C. fresh mushrooms, chopped
- ☐ 3 C. zucchini, chopped
- ☐ 2 C. bell peppers, seeded, chopped
- ☐ ½ tsp. dried thyme
- ☐ ½ tsp. dried marjoram
- ☐ Salt and ground black pepper
- ☐ ¾ C. vegetable broth
- ☐ 2 tsp. fresh lemon juice

For the Rolls:

- ☐ 8 cabbage leaves
- ☐ 8 oz. tomato sauce

Directions

1. Preheat oven to 400°F. Spray a 13x9-inch casserole dish with baking spray.
2. For the filling, add mushrooms and the remaining ingredients except for lemon juice to a large saucepan over medium heat and cook until boiling.
3. Immediately turn the heat low and cook for 5 minutes with a cover, then set aside.
4. Add lemon juice and mix to incorporate.
5. Meanwhile, place cabbage leaves into a large pot of boiling water for 2-4 minutes.
6. Drain the cabbage leaves thoroughly and arrange them on a smooth surface.
7. In each leaf, cut a V shape by cutting the thick vein.
8. Before filling, overlap the cut ends of each leaf.
9. Divide the filling mixture over each leaf evenly.
10. Roll thoroughly to enclose the filling and secure the rolls with toothpicks.
11. Put 6 tbsp. of tomato sauce in the bottom of a baking pan.
12. Arrange the rolls over the sauce and top with the remaining sauce.
13. Cover the casserole dish and bake for 15 min. Take it out from the oven and enjoy.

EGGPLANT
Parmesan

 PREP 20 MIN   COOK 55 MIN    SERVES 8

Ingredients

- [ ] 1 C. unsweetened almond milk
- [ ] 1/3 C. almond flour
- [ ] 4 C. cornflakes
- [ ] 1 C. raw cashews
- [ ] 1/3 C. nutritional yeast
- [ ] 1 tbsp. Italian seasoning
- [ ] 1½ tsp. salt
- [ ] 2 lb. eggplant, cut into ½-in thick slices
- [ ] 3 C. marinara sauce
- [ ] 3 C. vegan mozzarella cheese, shredded
- [ ] ½ C. vegan Parmesan cheese, shredded
- [ ] ¼ C. fresh basil chopped

Directions

1. Preheat your oven to 400°F. Spray two large baking sheets with baking spray.
2. In a small bowl, whisk together almond milk & flour and transfer to a shallow dish.
3. In a high-powered blender, add cornflakes, cashews, nutritional yeast, Italian seasoning, and salt and process to form a crumbly mixture.
4. Transfer the crumb mixture to a second shallow dish.
5. Dip each eggplant piece into the flour mixture and coat with the crumb mixture.
6. Arrange the eggplant pieces onto the baking sheets in a single layer.
7. Bake for 35 minutes, flipping once after 20 min, and take them out of the oven.
8. Again, set your oven to 400°F.
9. Spread ½ cup of marinara sauce in the bottom of a 13x9-inch casserole dish.
10. Arrange half of the baked eggplant slices over the sauce, overlapping slightly.
11. Top with half the remaining marinara sauce and half the mozzarella cheese.
12. Repeat with remaining eggplant, marinara, and mozzarella cheese.
13. Bake for about 20 minutes. Remove the casserole dish from the oven and sprinkle the top with parmesan cheese. Garnish with basil, and enjoy.

Lentils & Carrots Stew

SERVES 6

Ingredients

- [ ] 1½ tbsp. olive oil
- [ ] ½ C. onion, chopped
- [ ] 1 tsp. fresh ginger, minced
- [ ] 2 cloves garlic, minced
- [ ] 1½ C. tomato, finely chopped
- [ ] 1½ C. carrots, chopped
- [ ] 1½ C. green lentils, rinsed
- [ ] 3 C. vegetable broth
- [ ] 1 C. fresh parsley, chopped
- [ ] Salt and ground black pepper

Directions

1. Heat the oil over medium heat in a pot and sauté onion & carrots for 5 minutes.
2. Add the tomatoes, ginger, garlic, salt, pepper, and sauté for 3-4 minutes.
3. Add broth & lentils and cook until boiling.
4. Turn the heat low and simmer, covered, for 25-30 minutes.
5. Add fresh parsley on top.
6. Enjoy hot.

Barley & Beans Stew

SERVES 8

Ingredients

- [ ] 2 tbsp. olive oil
- [ ] 2 carrots, peeled and chopped
- [ ] 1 large onion, chopped
- [ ] 2 celery stalks, chopped
- [ ] 2 cloves garlic, minced
- [ ] 1 C. barley
- [ ] 1 C. cannellini beans
- [ ] 2 C. mushrooms, finely chopped
- [ ] 5-6 C. vegetable broth
- [ ] 1 C. fresh parsley and dill, chopped
- [ ] Salt and ground black pepper

Directions

1. Heat the oil over medium heat in a large pan and sauté the carrots, onion, celery, mushrooms, garlic for 5 minutes.
2. Add the barley, beans, salt, tomatoes, and broth and cook until boiling.
3. Turn the heat to low and simmer, covered for about 40 minutes.
4. Add parsley, dill, and pepper. Enjoy hot.

HOMEMADE
Ratatouille

 PREP 20 MIN COOK 45 MIN  SERVES 4

Ingredients

- [ ] 6 oz. tomato paste
- [ ] 3 tbsp. olive oil, divided
- [ ] ½ of medium onion, chopped
- [ ] 3 tbsp. garlic, minced
- [ ] Salt and ground black pepper
- [ ] 1 tbsp. fresh lemon juice
- [ ] ¾ C. water

- [ ] 2 yellow squash, sliced into circles thinly
- [ ] 2 eggplant, sliced into circles thinly
- [ ] 5-7 tomatoes, sliced into thin circles
- [ ] 1 tsp. fresh thyme leaves, minced
- [ ] 1 tsp. fresh rosemary, minced
- [ ] Fresh basil leaves for garnishing

Directions

1. For preheating, set your oven to 375°F.
2. Add the tomato paste, one tablespoon of oil, onion, garlic, salt, and pepper to a bowl and blend thoroughly.
3. Spread the tomato paste mixture in the bottom of a 10x10-inch baking dish.
4. Arrange alternating vegetable slices, starting at the outer edge of the baking dish and working concentrically towards the center.
5. Drizzle the vegetables with the remaining oil and lemon juice.
6. Sprinkle the top with salt and pepper, followed by fresh herbs.
7. Arrange a piece of baking paper over the vegetables.
8. Bake for about 45 minutes.
9. Garnish with fresh basil leaves. Enjoy hot.

VEGETARIAN
Pie

 PREP 20 MIN   COOK 50 MIN  SERVES 8

Ingredients

- ☐ Non-stick baking spray
- ☐ 1 9-inch premade vegan pie crust
- ☐ 1 tbsp. olive oil
- ☐ Salt and ground black pepper
- ☐ 1 large onion, chopped
- ☐ 3 tomatoes, peeled and sliced
- ☐ 2 small zucchini, sliced into rings
- ☐ Fresh parsley for garnishing

- ☐ 1 bell pepper, seeded and chopped
- ☐ 2 cloves garlic, minced
- ☐ 1 tsp. dried oregano
- ☐ 2 tsp. red chili powder
- ☐ 2½ C. cooked or canned green peas
- ☐ 1 C. shredded plant-based non-dairy mozzarella cheese
- ☐ 3/4 cup plant-based mayonnaise

Directions

1. Preheat oven to 375 °F. Lightly grease a shallow baking dish with baking spray and place a pie crust.
2. Use a paper towel to pat dry the tomatoes to ensure that most excess juice is out.
3. Heat the oil in a large wok over medium heat. Sauté the onion, bell pepper, and zucchini for 3-4 minutes.
4. Add drained green peas, garlic, oregano, and spices and sauté for 2 minutes.
5. Layer the zucchini mixture on the bottom of the pie crust.
6. Combine the cheese and mayonnaise together and smooth over the top of the pie.
7. Bake for 45 minutes.
8. Remove the pie from the oven and set it aside for 5 minutes before serving.
9. Garnish with fresh parsley and enjoy.

Sweet Potato & Chickpeas Stew

SERVES 4

Ingredients

- [ ] 1 tsp. olive oil
- [ ] 7 oz. full-fat coconut milk
- [ ] 1 small onion, chopped
- [ ] 2 cloves garlic, finely chopped
- [ ] 1 can 15 oz. diced tomatoes, with juice
- [ ] 1 can 15 oz. chickpeas drained & rinsed
- [ ] 1 small sweet potato, peeled and cubed
- [ ] 1 tsp. curry powder
- [ ] ½ tsp. chili powder
- [ ] Salt and ground black pepper
- [ ] Parsley and vegan yogurt for topping

Directions

1. In a pot, sauté onion and garlic in olive oil for 4-5 minutes over medium heat.
2. Add diced tomatoes and spices. Then, add chickpeas, sweet potato, & coconut milk.
3. Once boiling, turn the heat to medium-low & simmer, uncovered for 35-40 min.
4. Garnish with parsley and serve with yogurt if desired. Enjoy hot.

Kidney Beans Curry

SERVES 6

Ingredients

- [ ] 4 tbsp. olive oil
- [ ] 1 medium onion, finely chopped
- [ ] 2 cloves garlic, minced
- [ ] 2 tbsp. fresh ginger, minced
- [ ] 1 tsp. ground cumin
- [ ] ½ tsp. ground turmeric
- [ ] ¼ tsp. cayenne pepper
- [ ] Salt and ground black pepper
- [ ] 2 large tomatoes, finely chopped
- [ ] 3 C. cooked red kidney beans
- [ ] 2 C. water

Directions

1. Heat the oil over medium-low heat in a large pot, and cook the onion, garlic, ginger, and spices for 5-6 minutes.
2. Blend in the tomatoes, beans, & water and cook until boiling over high heat.
3. Turn the heat to medium and simmer for 10-15 minutes.
4. Enjoy hot.

Vegan Mushroom Burger

SERVES 2

Ingredients

- [ ] 2 vegan multigrain burger buns
- [ ] 1 tsp. olive oil
- [ ] Half of a small onion, chopped
- [ ] 2 cloves garlic, finely chopped
- [ ] 1 medium tomato, sliced
- [ ] Half of a small cucumber, sliced
- [ ] A few slices of red bell pepper
- [ ] A few thin slices of eggplant
- [ ] ½ C. sliced mushrooms
- [ ] 4 Romaine lettuce leaves
- [ ] 2 pinches of microgreens
- [ ] 2 tbsp. shredded carrot
- [ ] 4 tbsp. hummus

Directions

1. In a skillet, sauté onion, carrot, and garlic in olive oil for 4 min. over medium heat.
2. Add eggplant, mushrooms, salt, and pepper, and saute until eggplant is soft.
3. Put hummus on each half of the bun.
4. Add lettuce & arrange veggies in layers.

Roasted Brussels Sprouts

SERVES 6

Ingredients

- [ ] 1½ lb. Brussels sprouts, halved
- [ ] 1 medium onion, chopped
- [ ] 1 C. carrot, chopped
- [ ] 3 tbsp. extra virgin olive oil
- [ ] ¾ tsp. salt
- [ ] ½ tsp. freshly ground black pepper
- [ ] 1 tbsp. balsamic vinegar
- [ ] 1 tsp. honey
- [ ] 1/2 cup of water

Directions

1. In a wok, heat 1 tbsp. of oil over medium heat and sauté onion & carrot for 5 min.
2. Add Brussels sprouts with 2 tbsp of oil, salt, and pepper. Roast, stirring once halfway through, about 10 minutes.
3. Pour 1/2 cup of water over the sprouts and cook for another 8 minutes until the water evaporates. Drizzle the balsamic vinegar and honey over the roasted Brussels sprouts and cook for 2 min.

CHICKPEAS
Falafels

 PREP 20 MIN  COOK 30 MIN  SERVES 8

Ingredients

- ☐ 2½ C. dried chickpeas, soaked overnight
- ☐ 8 C. water
- ☐ ½ bunch fresh parsley, stemmed
- ☐ ¼ bunch fresh mint, stemmed
- ☐ ¼ bunch of fresh cilantro
- ☐ 5 cloves garlic, peeled & halved
- ☐ 1 onion, peeled and chopped
- ☐ 2 tsp. ground cumin
- ☐ 2 tsp. ground coriander
- ☐ 1 tsp. paprika
- ☐ 1 tsp. baking soda
- ☐ 1 tbsp. sesame seeds toasted
- ☐ Salt and ground black pepper

For the salad:
- ☐ 8 C. mixed lettuce, washed
- ☐ 4 tomatoes, sliced
- ☐ 2 lemons, sliced

Directions

1. For the falafels, drain the chickpeas, place them on a paper towel baking sheet, and cover them with another layer of paper towels. Let them dry for 2 hours.
2. For preheating: set your oven to 350°F.
3. Lay out baking paper on a baking tray.
4. Put the chickpeas and remaining falafel ingredients into a food mixer and process to form a smooth mixture.
5. Shape the mixture into 16 falafels and lay them on the baking tray.
6. Spray the falafels with baking spray and bake in the oven for 25-30 minutes.
7. Place falafels and salad ingredients on serving plates.
8. Serve with Lemon Tahini Sauce. Enjoy immediately.

TOFU BROCCOLI
Stir Fry

 PREP 10 MIN    COOK 20 MIN    SERVES 2

Ingredients

- ☐ 1 (14-oz.) package of firm tofu, pressed, drained, and cubed
- ☐ 2 tbsp. olive oil, divided
- ☐ 2 C. broccoli florets
- ☐ 1 tsp. garlic powder
- ☐ Salt and ground black pepper
- ☐ 2 tsp cornstarch, divided
- ☐ ¼ C. water

For the stir-fry sauce:

- ☐ 2 tbsp. soy sauce
- ☐ 1 tbsp. sesame oil
- ☐ 1 tbsp. maple syrup
- ☐ 1 tbsp. rice wine vinegar or lime juice
- ☐ 3-4 cloves garlic, finely minced
- ☐ ½ tbsp. fresh ginger, finely minced

Directions

1. In an airtight container, add 1 tsp. of cornstarch, garlic powder, salt, and pepper and mix well. Add tofu, seal the container, and toss gently to coat it completely.
2. Combine all of your stir-fry sauce ingredients, including the remaining 1 tsp. of corn starch and water, and whisk well.
3. In a large skillet, heat 1 tbsp. of oil over medium-high heat.
4. Add your tofu pieces in one even layer and cook for about 3 minutes on each side or until golden.
5. Add your broccoli to the pan and stir frequently to help cook the broccoli evenly.
6. Pour in your stir-fry sauce and start to stir it into your tofu and vegetables, making sure that everything is evenly coated and that the sauce is thickening.
7. Remove from the heat and serve with cooked rice and sesame seeds.

RICE & LENTIL
Loaf

 PREP 10 MIN   COOK 20 MIN   SERVES 2

Ingredients

- ☐ 3 C. water
- ☐ 1 tbsp olive oil
- ☐ 1 C. brown rice
- ☐ 1 C. brown lentils
- ☐ ½ C. red bell pepper chopped
- ☐ 2 medium yellow onion, chopped
- ☐ 1 celery stalk, chopped
- ☐ 6 cremini mushrooms, chopped
- ☐ 6 freshly chopped garlic
- ☐ 1 ½ C. old-fashioned rolled oats
- ☐ ½ C. walnuts, finely chopped
- ☐ 2 cans tomato paste (12 ounces)
- ☐ 1 C. pecans or walnuts, chopped
- ☐ 2 tsp. fresh rosemary, minced
- ☐ 2 tsp. fresh thyme, minced
- ☐ 1 tsp. Italian seasoning

Directions

1. In a pot, add water, rice, lentils, salt, and Italian seasoning, and cook over medium-high heat until boiling. Turn the heat low and cook, covered, for 45 minutes. Then, set aside and cover for at least 10 minutes.
2. Preheat your oven to 350 °F. Line a 9x5-inch loaf pan with bakery paper.
3. In a wok, heat the oil over medium heat and sauté the onion, celery, mushrooms, pepper, and garlic for 4-5 minutes. Set aside to cool slightly.
4. Add the oats, walnuts, tomato paste, and fresh herbs to a large bowl and mix well.
5. Add the rice mixture and vegetables and mix well.
6. In a blender, add the mixture and pulse until just a chunky mixture forms.
7. Place the mixture into the prepared loaf pan, cover with foil, and bake for 40 min.
8. Uncover and bake for 15 more minutes, then take it out to cool.
9. Carefully invert the loaf to a platter, cut it into serving portions, and enjoy.

BLACK BEAN
Veggie Tacos

 PREP 10 MIN   COOK 20 MIN   🍽 SERVES 4

Ingredients

- ☐ 2 tbsp. creamy Tahini sauce
- ☐ 2 tsp. black sesame seeds
- ☐ **For the Tortillas:**
- ☐ ½ C. dry black beans, rinsed
- ☐ ¾ C. water
- ☐ ½ tsp. salt

- ☐ **For the Tacos:**
- ☐ 1 avocado, peeled, pitted and sliced
- ☐ 1 large tomato, sliced
- ☐ ½ C. fresh baby greens
- ☐ ¼ C. pomegranate seeds
- ☐ 2 scallions, sliced

Directions

1. In a large bowl of water, soak the beans for at least 12 hours.
2. Drain the beans and rinse well.
3. In a blender, add beans, water, and salt, and process to form a smooth mixture.
4. Transfer the beans puree into a bowl.
5. Heat a non-stick wok over medium heat.
6. Add 1/4 C. of the mixture and wait for around 5-10 seconds.
7. Spread the mixture into a 7-inch circle with a metal spoon and cook for 3 minutes.
8. Carefully flip the tortilla and cook for another 2 minutes.
9. Transfer the tortilla onto a cooling rack to cool completely.
10. Repeat with the remaining mixture.
11. Arrange the tortillas on serving plates and divide the avocado, tomato, greens, pomegranate seeds, and scallion into each tortilla.
12. Sprinkle sesame seeds and add Tahini sauce. Enjoy immediately.

BLACK BEANS
Enchiladas

 PREP 20 MIN COOK 25 MIN  SERVES 6

Ingredients

- ☐ 1 tbsp. avocado oil
- ☐ 1 medium yellow onion, chopped
- ☐ 2 cloves garlic, minced
- ☐ 3 tbsp. red chili powder
- ☐ 2 tsp. cumin powder
- ☐ 1 tsp. salt
- ☐ 2 C. canned black beans
- ☐ 2 C. tomato puree
- ☐ 8 oz. vegan cheese, shredded
- ☐ ½ C. fresh cilantro, chopped
- ☐ 1 jalapeño, seeded and chopped
- ☐ 12 (5½-inch) corn tortillas, warmed

Directions

1. In a wok, heat oil over medium heat and sauté the onion and garlic for 3 minutes.
2. Add the chili powder, cumin, salt, and sauté for another 2 minutes.
3. Add in beans and tomato puree and cook until boiling.
4. Turn the heat to low, mash the beans with a potato masher, and simmer for 5 min.
5. Remove the bean mixture from the heat and strain it through a fine-mesh strainer, reserving the sauce in a bowl.
6. In another large bowl, add the strained bean mixture, 4 oz. of the vegan cheese, cilantro, and jalapeño pepper, and mix well.
7. Meanwhile, preheat your oven to 350°F.
8. On the bottom of a baking dish, spread ½ C. of the sauce.
9. Arrange the tortillas on a smooth surface. Divide the bean mixture between each tortilla and roll it up tightly. Place them over the sauce in the baking dish.
10. Place the remaining sauce over the enchiladas, followed by the remaining cheese.
11. Cover the baking dish with a piece of foil and bake for 20 minutes, then remove the foil and bake for 2 more minutes. Enjoy warm.

RICE & VEGGIE
Paella

 PREP 15 MIN  COOK 30 MIN 🍴 SERVES 5

Ingredients

- ☐ 3 tbsp. olive oil, divided
- ☐ 4 C. vegetable broth
- ☐ 1 tsp. saffron threads
- ☐ 1 medium onion, diced
- ☐ 1 red bell pepper, cut into strips
- ☐ 5 cloves garlic, minced
- ☐ ½ C. tomato, diced
- ☐ 6-8 asparagus spears, cut in half
- ☐ ½ C. broccoli, halved
- ☐ 1 ½ C. Bomba rice (or Arborio rice)
- ☐ 1 tsp. smoked paprika
- ☐ ½ tsp. sweet paprika
- ☐ 1 tsp. sea salt and black pepper
- ☐ 2 sprigs fresh thyme (or 1 tsp. dry)
- ☐ ¾ cup frozen peas, thawed
- ☐ A few slices of lemon to garnish

Directions

1. Add vegetable broth to a medium saucepan over medium-high heat. Break up the saffron and add it to the broth, cooking for 1 minute.
2. Heat 2 tbsp. of oil in a 12-inch Paella pan over medium heat. Add the onions, bell pepper, broccoli, and garlic. Sauté for 5 min. until softened and lightly browned.
3. Now add the tomatoes, asparagus, and paprika. Sauté for a minute.
4. Add rice and the remaining 1 tbsp. of oil to the pan. Stir to coat well. Cook for 1 minute to toast the rice and incorporate flavors lightly.
5. Add the fresh thyme and slowly pour in broth. Add salt and pepper. Turn the heat to medium-high and bring the broth to a heavy simmer for 1-2 minutes.
6. Turn the heat to medium and bring to a mild simmer. Simmer for 15-20 minutes or until the golden rice crust is formed.
7. Remove the pan from the heat. Add the peas to the top, cover the pan with foil, and let the paella rest for 5 minutes. Top with fresh-cut lemon. Enjoy!

Veggie Fried Rice

SERVES 4

Ingredients

- ☐ 3 tbsp. vegetable oil
- ☐ ½ C. onion, chopped
- ☐ 2 tsp. garlic, chopped
- ☐ ½ C. carrots, peeled and chopped
- ☐ ½ C. fresh green peas, shelled
- ☐ ¼ C. Canned or frozen corn
- ☐ 4 C. cooked white rice
- ☐ 1 tbsp. sesame oil, toasted
- ☐ 1 tbsp. soy sauce
- ☐ Salt and ground white pepper

Directions

1. In a wok, heat oil over medium heat and stir-fry the onion and garlic for about 1 minute.
2. Add carrots and peas and stir-fry for another 2-3 minutes.
3. Add the cooked rice, salt, white pepper, soy sauce, and sesame oil and cook for 1-2 minutes, tossing frequently.
4. Enjoy hot.

Pasta with Mushrooms

SERVES 4

Ingredients

- ☐ 1 (8-oz.) package vegan pasta
- ☐ 2 tbsp. olive oil
- ☐ 1 tbsp. garlic, minced
- ☐ 1 tbsp. dried oregano, crushed
- ☐ 2 C. fresh mushroom, sliced
- ☐ Salt and ground black pepper
- ☐ 2 tbsp. fresh parsley, chopped
- ☐ 2 tbsp. vegan cheese, shredded

Directions

1. In a large-sized pot of lightly salted boiling water, cook the pasta for 8-10 minutes.
2. Drain the pasta well.
3. Heat oil over medium heat in a large-sized wok and sauté the garlic and herbs for about 1 minute.
4. Add mushrooms and cook for 7 minutes.
5. Add the pasta, salt and pepper and cook for 2-3 minutes.
6. Add parsley and cheese on top. Enjoy.

TOFU
Pad Thai

 PREP 20 MIN   COOK 15 MIN    SERVES 6

Ingredients

- ☐ 1 lb. vegan rice noodles
- ☐ 1½ C. peanut butter
- ☐ 1 C. coconut milk
- ☐ 1/3 C. water
- ☐ 1/3 C. soy sauce
- ☐ 1/3 C. fresh lemon juice
- ☐ 2 tbsp. peanut oil
- ☐ 14 oz of extra-firm tofu

- ☐ 1 tsp. garlic powder
- ☐ 1 tbsp. paprika
- ☐ ¼ tsp. cayenne pepper
- ☐ 2 tbsp. vegetable oil
- ☐ 1 lb. mung bean sprouts
- ☐ ½ C. peanuts, chopped
- ☐ ¼ C. fresh cilantro, chopped
- ☐ 1 lemon, cut into wedges

Directions

1. In a large bowl of hot water, soak the rice noodles for 5 minutes.
2. Drain the noodles and set aside.
3. For the sauce, mix the peanut butter, coconut milk, water, soy sauce, lemon juice, peanut oil, garlic powder, paprika, and cayenne pepper in a small saucepan over medium heat and cook for 4 minutes, stirring continuously.
4. Take the pot off the heat and set it aside.
5. Heat vegetable oil over medium-low heat in a large wok. Add the drained tofu and brown on each side for a minute, then cook it for about 5-7 minutes.
6. Add the noodles and cook for 2 minutes, stirring continuously.
7. Stir in sauce, bean sprouts, peanuts, and cilantro, and cook for about 5 minutes.
8. Garnish with lemon wedges, peanuts, and cilantro, and enjoy immediately.

TOMATO
Pizza

 PREP 15 MIN  COOK 13 MIN  SERVES 6

Ingredients

- ☐ 12 oz. refrigerated vegan pizza dough
- ☐ 1 C. fresh basil leaves
- ☐ 6 cloves garlic
- ☐ 3 tbsp. olive oil, divided
- ☐ 4 oz. vegan parmesan cheese, shredded
- ☐ 2 (6-oz.) heirloom tomatoes, cut into ¼-inch thick slices
- ☐ Salt and ground black pepper

Directions

1. For preheating, set your oven to 500°F. If using a pizza stone, place it on the bottom rack for at least 15 minutes.
2. In a mini food processor, add ½ C. of the basil, garlic, and oil and process to form a smooth mixture.
3. Place the dough on a lightly floured surface and roll into a 14-inch round. Fold the edges to form a more crusty crust.
4. With a fork, pierce the surface of the dough.
5. If using a pizza stone, quickly transfer the dough to the stone, add the sauce, cheese, and tomatoes, sprinkle with black pepper, and put it in the oven.
6. Bake for about 5 minutes, then rotate and bake for another 8 minutes or until the crust is golden and the cheese is melted.
7. If you are not using a stone, roll out the dough on a lightly greased baking sheet. Add sauce, cheese, and toppings, and bake for 12 minutes.
8. Set the pizza aside for 5 minutes before slicing.
9. Garnish with fresh basil, cut into slices, and enjoy.

05

CHAPTER FIVE

Kitchen Staple Sensations

Greek Dressing

- 1 clove garlic, minced
- ¼ C. olive oil
- 2 tbsp. fresh lemon juice
- 1 tsp. dried oregano, crushed
- ¼ tsp. salt
- ¼ tsp. ground black pepper

1. In a bowl, add all ingredients and whisk to incorporate thoroughly.
2. Transfer the dressing to an airtight jar and store it in the refrigerator before using.

Strawberry Dressing

SERVES 4

- ½ C. fresh strawberries, hulled and sliced
- ½ C. olive oil
- 2 tbsp. balsamic vinegar
- 1 tsp. pure maple syrup
- 1 tsp. mustard
- 1 tsp. salt
- 1 tsp. ground black pepper

1. In a high-powered blender, add strawberries and process to form a puree.
2. Add remaining ingredients and process to form a smooth mixture.
3. Transfer the dressing to an airtight jar and store it in the refrigerator before using.

Cilantro & Avocado Dressing

SERVES 8

- ¾ C. fresh cilantro, chopped
- ½ of medium avocado, peeled, pitted and chopped
- 2 medium onions, chopped
- 1 clove garlic, chopped
- ½ tsp. salt
- 1 /3 C. avocado oil
- 2 tbsp. fresh lime juice
- ¼ C. unsweetened coconut milk
- ½ tsp. ground black pepper

1. In a high-powered blender, add all ingredients and process to form a smooth mixture.
2. Transfer the dressing to an airtight jar and store it in the refrigerator.

Balsamic Vinaigrette

SERVES 8

- 2 tbsp. maple syrup
- 1 tbsp. Dijon mustard
- 1 tsp. salt and black pepper
- 1 large garlic clove, minced
- ¼ C. balsamic vinegar
- ¾ C. extra virgin olive oil

1. In a small mixing bowl, whisk together the maple syrup, garlic, balsamic, mustard, oil, salt & pepper.
2. Store in a jar with a lid and refrigerate.
3. Shake well before serving.

French Dressing

- 1 small onion, chopped
- 1½ C. olive oil
- 1 C. ketchup
- ¾ C. Erythritol
- ½ C. balsamic vinegar
- 1 tsp. paprika
- ½ tsp. salt

1. In a blender, place onion and remaining ingredients and process to form a smooth mixture.
2. Enjoy immediately.

Caesar Dressing

SERVES 8

- 2 tsp. capers
- ¼ C. Dijon mustard
- ½ C. Vegan Mayonnaise
- 2-3 tbsp. fresh lemon juice
- 1-2 tbsp. olive oil
- 1-2 tsp. maple syrup
- 4-5 cloves garlic, minced
- Salt & ground black pepper
- ½ C. vegan Parmigiano, grated

1. In a large bowl, mix capers, brining juice, garlic, salt, and pepper. Use a fork to mash the ingredients together.
2. Add lemon juice, Dijon mustard, mayonnaise, Parmigiano, oil, maple syrup, and whisk until well combined. Continue to stir until completely emulsified. Enjoy.

Chimichurri Sauce

SERVES 6

- ½ C. olive oil
- 1/3 C. balsamic vinegar
- 4 cloves garlic, minced
- ½ C. fresh parsley, chopped
- ½ C. fresh cilantro, chopped
- 1 tbsp. fresh oregano, chopped
- ½ tsp. red pepper flakes
- ½ C. red onion, chopped
- Salt, as desired

1. In a food processor, add all the ingredients and pulse 2-3 times to mix.
2. Season with salt to taste.
3. The sauce is ready to use.
4. You can store in the refrigerator 1-3 days.

Homemade Salad Dressing

SERVES 6

- 4 tbsp. virgin olive oil
- 4 tbsp. fresh lime juice
- 4 tbsp. maple syrup
- 1 tsp. cumin
- ½ tsp. chili powder
- 1 tsp. salt & black pepper
- 2 tbsp. fresh cilantro, chopped

1. Whisk together the olive oil, lime juice, maple syrup, cumin, chili powder, salt, and pepper in a small mixing bowl until well combined and emulsified.
2. Add cilantro before serving.

Peanut Butter Sauce

SERVES 3

- ½ C. creamy peanut butter
- 2 tbsp. low-sodium soy sauce
- 1 tbsp. maple syrup
- 2 tbsp. fresh lime juice
- 1 tsp. chile-garlic sauce
- ¼ C. water

1. In a bowl, place all the ingredients and whisk to incorporate thoroughly.
2. Enjoy immediately.

Cranberry Sauce

SERVES 8

- 1 cinnamon stick
- 3 whole allspice berries
- 3 whole cloves
- 1 C. water
- ½ C. orange juice
- 2 C. fresh or frozen cranberries
- 1½ C. maple syrup
- 2 wide strips of orange zest for serving (optional)

1. In a spice bag, wrap cloves, cinnamon, allspice berries.
2. In a pot, add a spice bag, water, juice, and cranberries over medium heat and cook for 9-10 minutes.
3. Add maple syrup and cook 5 minutes, continuously stirring.
4. Take it out of the heat and discard the spice bag.
5. Refrigerate to chill for 8 hours before serving.

BBQ Sauce

SERVES 12

- 16 oz. tomato sauce
- 2 tbsp. tomato paste
- ½ C. apple cider vinegar
- 5 tbsp. maple syrup
- 1 tbsp. fresh lemon juice
- ½ tbsp. Dijon mustard
- ½ tbsp. onion powder
- ½ tbsp. ground black pepper
- 1 tsp. paprika

1. In a medium pot, blend together all ingredients over medium-high heat and cook until boiling.
2. Turn the heat to low and simmer for around 30 minutes or until desired thickness.
3. Remove from heat. Cool completely, then cover and store in the refrigerator up to 2 weeks.

Basil Pesto

SERVES 16

- 2 C. fresh basil
- 3 tbsp. pine nuts
- 3 cloves garlic, chopped
- 2 tbsp. fresh lemon juice
- 3-4 tbsp. nutritional yeast
- 2-3 tbsp. olive oil
- 3-6 tbsp. water

1. Place basil, nuts, lemon juice, garlic, nutritional yeast in a food processor. Process until a chunky mixture is formed.
2. Slowly add in oil and process to form a smooth mixture.
3. Now, add the water and process it thoroughly.

70

Turmeric Tahini Sauce

SERVES 4

- ¼ C. tahini
- 2 cloves garlic, peeled
- 3 tbsp. olive oil
- 3 tbsp. water
- 1½ tbsp. fresh lemon juice
- 1/3 tsp. ground turmeric

1. Place all the ingredients in a high-speed blender and process until creamy. Add salt and ground black pepper as desired.
2. Sprinkle with 1 tsp. sesame seeds and serve.

Cashew Mayo

SERVES 5

- 1 C. raw, unsalted cashews
- ½ C. water
- 1 tbsp. nutritional yeast
- 1 tsp. fresh lemon juice
- 1 tsp. dijon mustard
- 1/8 tsp. salt

1. In a bowl of water, soak the cashews overnight or about 12 hours.
2. Drain the cashews thoroughly.
3. Add all the ingredients to a food processor and process at high speed to form a smooth and creamy sauce.
4. Enjoy immediately or keep it in the fridge in a lidded container for up to 3 days.

Beet Hummus

SERVES 6

- 15 oz. canned beets, drained
- 2 C. cooked chickpeas
- 1 small clove garlic, peeled
- 3 tbsp. tahini
- 1-1½ tbsp. fresh lemon juice
- ½ tsp. ground cumin
- ½ tsp. ground coriander
- ½ tsp. sumac
- 1-2 tbsp. olive oil
- 2 tbsp. fresh parsley

1. In a food processor, add all ingredients except for olive oil and process to form a smooth mixture. Add salt to taste.
2. While the motor is running, add 2 ice cubes or fresh water and process them thoroughly.
3. Transfer the beet hummus into a bowl and drizzle with oil, garnish with parsley and enjoy.

Chickpeas Hummus

SERVES 12

- 3 C. cooked chickpeas
- ½ C. smooth tahini
- 2 tbsp. extra-virgin olive oil
- 2 tbsp. fresh lemon juice
- 1 garlic clove, chopped
- ½ tsp. sea salt
- Pinch of cayenne pepper

1. In a blender, place the chickpeas, tahini, olive oil, lemon juice, garlic, and salt. Blend until very smooth, adding water if needed.
2. Transfer to a serving plate and sprinkle with cayenne pepper and fresh parsley.

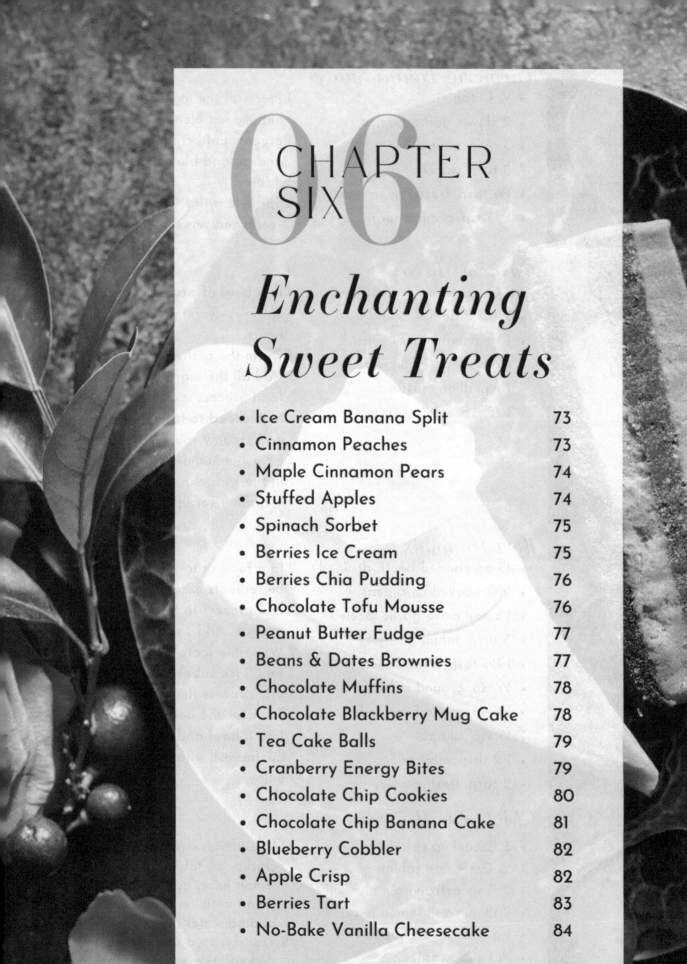

CHAPTER SIX

06

Enchanting Sweet Treats

Ice Cream Banana Split

SERVES 2

Ingredients

- ☐ 2 medium bananas, peeled and halved
- ☐ 4 scoops vegan ice cream
- ☐ 3 tbsp. vegan chocolate sauce
- ☐ ½ C. fresh cherries
- ☐ 2 tbsp. whipped coconut cream
- ☐ 2 tbsp. walnuts, chopped

Directions

1. Arrange the banana halves onto a platter.
2. Top each with ice cream, followed by chocolate sauce and coconut cream.
3. Garnish with cherries and walnuts, and enjoy.

Cinnamon Peaches

SERVES 4

Ingredients

- ☐ Non-stick baking spray
- ☐ 2 large peaches, halved and pitted
- ☐ 1/8 tsp. ground cinnamon
- ☐ 4 fresh mint leaves
- ☐ Whipped coconut cream for garnishing

Directions

1. For preheating, set your grill to medium-high heat. Grease the grill grate with baking spray.
2. Arrange the peach halves onto the grill and cut the side down.
3. Grill for around 3-5 minutes per side.
4. Sprinkle with cinnamon and garnish with whipped coconut cream and mint leaves.
5. Enjoy.

Maple Cinnamon Pears

SERVES 4

Ingredients

- [ ] 4 medium pears, halved and cored
- [ ] ¼ tsp. ground cinnamon
- [ ] ½ C. maple syrup
- [ ] 1 tsp. vanilla extract

Directions

1. For preheating, set your oven to 375°F. Line a baking tray with bakery paper.
2. Arrange the pear halves onto the baking tray, cut side upwards, and sprinkle with cinnamon.
3. Add maple syrup and vanilla extract into a small bowl and whisk to incorporate.
4. Reserve about 2 tbsp. of the maple syrup mixture.
5. Put the remaining maple syrup mixture over the pears.
6. Bake for around 25 minutes.
7. Remove it from the oven and drizzle the pears with the reserved maple syrup mixture.
8. Enjoy warm.

Stuffed Apples

SERVES 6

Ingredients

- [ ] 6 small apples, tops removed
- [ ] ¾ C. rolled oats
- [ ] ¾ C. walnuts, chopped
- [ ] 3 tbsp. maple syrup
- [ ] 1 tsp. ground cinnamon
- [ ] ¼ tsp. ground ginger
- [ ] ¾ C. water

Directions

1. For preheating: set your oven to 350°F.
2. With a spoon, carefully scoop out the flesh inside the apples.
3. Put apples' flesh and remaining ingredients except for water into a bowl and mix to incorporate.
4. Stuff the apples with walnut mixture.
5. Arrange the apples into a baking pan.
6. Place the water in the baking pan.
7. Bake for about 30-40 minutes.
8. Take the baking pot out of the oven and set aside to cool slightly before enjoying.

Spinach Sorbet

SERVES 4

Ingredients

- [ ] 3 C. fresh spinach, torn
- [ ] 1 tbsp. fresh basil leaves
- [ ] ½ of avocado, peeled, pitted and chopped
- [ ] ¾ C. almond milk
- [ ] 20 drops of liquid stevia
- [ ] 1 tsp. almonds, chopped very finely
- [ ] 1 tsp. vanilla extract
- [ ] 1 C. ice cubes

Directions

1. In a blender, add all the ingredients and process until creamy and smooth.
2. Transfer into an ice cream maker and process according to the manufacturer's directions.
3. Transfer into an airtight container and freeze for at least 4-5 hours before enjoying.

Berries Ice Cream

SERVES 6

Ingredients

- [ ] ¼ C. cashews
- [ ] 2 C. fresh berries (strawberries,
- [ ] raspberries, blueberries)
- [ ] 1 avocado, peeled, pitted and chopped
- [ ] 10 dates, pitted and chopped
- [ ] 1¾ C. unsweetened almond milk
- [ ] 2 /3 C. water
- [ ] 1 tbsp. fresh lemon juice

Directions

1. In a bowl of water, soak the cashews for around 30 minutes. Drain thoroughly.
2. In a blender, add cashews and reaming ingredients and process to form a creamy and smooth mixture.
3. Transfer into an ice cream maker and process according to the manufacturer's directions.
4. Transfer into an airtight container and freeze for 4-5 hours before enjoying.
5. Garnish with fresh berries.

Acai Chia Pudding

 SERVES 4

Ingredients

- ☐ 1 C. chia seeds
- ☐ 3 C. unsweetened almond milk
- ☐ 6 tsp. acai powder
- ☐ 1 tsp. vanilla extract
- ☐ 2 tbsp. maple syrup
- ☐ 1 C. fresh mixed berries (blueberries, raspberries, blackberries)

Directions

1. Mix all the ingredients except for the berries in a bowl until well combined.
2. Place in the fridge and let sit for 2-4 hours until you have a thick texture.
3. Garnish with some fresh fruits.
4. Enjoy.

Chocolate Tofu Mousse

 SERVES 6

Ingredients

- ☐ 1 lb. firm tofu, drained
- ☐ ¼ C. unsweetened almond milk
- ☐ 2 tbsp. cacao powder
- ☐ 10-15 drops liquid stevia
- ☐ 1 tbsp. vanilla extract
- ☐ 1/2 C. fresh raspberries
- ☐ Fresh mint leaves for garnishing

Directions

1. In a blender, add all ingredients except the raspberries and process until creamy and smooth.
2. Transfer into serving bowls and refrigerate to chill for at least 2 hours before enjoying.
3. Garnish with strawberries, mint and enjoy!

Peanut Butter Fudge

SERVES 16

Ingredients

- [ ] 1½ C. creamy, salted peanut butter
- [ ] 1/3 C. coconut oil
- [ ] 2/3 C. coconut sugar
- [ ] ¼ C. vegan protein powder
- [ ] 1 tsp. vanilla extract
- [ ] Kosher salt for sprinkling

Directions

1. In a small pot, add peanut butter, coconut sugar, and coconut oil and cook over low heat until melted and smooth.
2. Put in protein powder and blend to form a smooth mixture.
3. Take off the heat & put in vanilla extract.
4. Place the fudge mixture into an 8x8-inch baking dish lined with baking paper and smooth the top surface with a spatula.
5. Freeze for about 30-45 minutes.
6. Carefully place the fudge onto a cutting board with the help of bakery paper.
7. Cut the fudge into squares, sprinkle with salt, and enjoy.

Beans & Dates Brownies

SERVES 12

Ingredients

- [ ] 2 C. cooked black beans
- [ ] 12 large dates, pitted and chopped
- [ ] 2 tbsp. almond butter
- [ ] 2 tbsp. quick rolled oats
- [ ] 2 tsp. vanilla extract
- [ ] ¼ C. cacao powder
- [ ] 1 tbsp. ground cinnamon

Directions

1. For preheating, set your oven to 350°F. Line a baking dish with baking paper.
2. In a food processor, add all the ingredients except the cacao powder and cinnamon and process to incorporate thoroughly and smooth.
3. Transfer the mixture to a large bowl.
4. Add the cacao powder and cinnamon and blend to incorporate.
5. Transfer the mixture to a prepared baking dish, smooth the top surface with a spatula, and bake for 30 minutes.
6. Take it out of the oven and cool completely. Cut brownies and enjoy.

Chocolate Muffins

SERVES 6

Ingredients

- [ ] 1 C. water
- [ ] 1 C. dates, pitted
- [ ] 1 C. oat flour
- [ ] ⅓ C. cacao powder
- [ ] 1 tbsp. baking powder
- [ ] ¼ C. unsweetened almond milk

Directions

1. Preheat your oven to 350°F. Line 6 cups of muffin pans with paper liners.
2. In a food processor, add water and dates and process to form a smooth mixture.
3. In a large bowl, blend flour, cacao powder, baking powder, and salt to taste.
4. Add the almond milk and date paste and whisk to incorporate thoroughly.
5. Transfer the mixture into muffin cups.
6. Bake for about 25 minutes.
7. Take the muffin pan out of the oven and place it on a wire rack to cool for 15 min.
8. Carefully invert the muffins onto the wire rack to cool completely before enjoying.

Chocolate Blackberry Mug Cake

SERVES 1

Ingredients

- [ ] 2 tbsp. almond flour
- [ ] 2 tbsp. coconut sugar
- [ ] 2 tsp. cacao powder
- [ ] 1/6 tsp. baking soda
- [ ] Pinch of salt
- [ ] 3 tbsp. coconut milk or water
- [ ] 1 tsp. coconut oil or canola oil
- [ ] 1/6 tsp. white vinegar
- [ ] 10 fresh blackberries

Directions

1. Blend the flour, coconut sugar, cacao powder, baking soda, and salt in a microwave-safe mug.
2. Add the water, oil, and vinegar and stir to form a smooth mixture.
3. Stir in the fresh blackberries.
4. Microwave on high setting for 1½-2 minutes or until set completely.
5. Take the mug from the microwave and set aside for 3-5 minutes.
6. Garnish with fresh mint and enjoy.

Tea Cake Balls

SERVES 18

Ingredients

- [ ] 1 tsp. pure vanilla extract
- [ ] 1 C. coconut oil, softened
- [ ] 2 C. almond flour
- [ ] 1/3 C. stevia
- [ ] 1/3 C. shredded coconut
- [ ] 1 C. walnuts, chopped

Directions

1. Preheat your oven to 350°F.
2. In a large bowl, add vanilla extract, stevia, coconut oil, and flour and whisk to form a smooth, creamy mixture.
3. Fold in walnuts.
4. Make 1-inch-sized balls from dough.
5. Arrange the dough onto a large-sized ungreased cookie sheet 2 inches apart.
6. Bake for 12 minutes.
7. Take the cookie sheet out of the oven and let it cool completely.
8. In a shallow dish, place the shredded coconut and roll each ball in it completely. Enjoy.

Cranberry Energy Bites

SERVES 16

Ingredients

- [ ] 1 ripe banana, peeled and mashed
- [ ] ¼ C. agave syrup
- [ ] ¼ C. almond butter, melted
- [ ] 1½ C. rolled quick oats
- [ ] 1/3 C. vegan protein powder
- [ ] 2 tsp. flaxseed meal
- [ ] 1 tsp. vanilla extract
- [ ] 1/3 C. unsweetened dried cranberries

Directions

1. Add the banana, agave syrup, and almond butter in a large bowl and blend to form a smooth mixture.
2. Add the oats, protein powder, flaxseed, and vanilla extract & mix to incorporate.
3. Gently fold in the cranberries.
4. Make small-sized balls from the mixture.
5. Arrange the balls on a paper-lined baking sheet and refrigerate for 1 hour before enjoying.

CHOCOLATE CHIP
Cookies

 PREP 15 MIN    COOK 8 MIN   SERVES 18

Ingredients

- ☐ 2 C. almond, oat, or spelt flour
- ☐ ¼ tsp. baking soda
- ☐ 1/4 tsp. salt
- ☐ 4 tbsp. agave nectar
- ☐ 1 tbsp. vanilla extract
- ☐ ¼ C. palm shortening or vegan butter
- ☐ ¼ C. vegan chocolate chips
- ☐ 2 tbsp. oat or coconut milk

Directions

1. For preheating: set your oven to 350°F.
2. Line a large-sized cookie sheet with a greased baking paper.
3. In a bowl, mix the flour, soda, and salt.
4. In another medium-sized bowl, add agave nectar, shortening, and vanilla extract and whisk until well combined.
5. Combine the oil mixture with the flour mixture and mix well.
6. Refrigerate for at least 2 hours.
7. With a tablespoon, place the mixture onto the cookie sheet 2 inches apart and slightly flatten the cookies.
8. Bake for 11 minutes on the center rack.
9. Remove the cookie sheet from the oven and place it on a cooling rack for 5-10 minutes.
10. Enjoy.

CHOCOLATE CHIP
Banana Cake

 PREP 15 MIN  COOK 40 MIN  SERVES 8

Ingredients

- ☐ 2 C. oat flour
- ☐ ½ C. almond flour
- ☐ ½ C. coconut sugar
- ☐ 1½ tsp. baking powder
- ☐ ¼ tsp. salt

- ☐ 3 medium ripe bananas, mashed
- ☐ ½ C. unsweetened almond milk
- ☐ ½ tbsp. apple cider vinegar
- ☐ 1 tsp. vanilla extract
- ☐ 1 C. vegan chocolate chips

Directions

1. For preheating: set your oven to 350°F.
2. Line a greased 8-inch loaf pan.
3. In a large bowl, put flour, sugar, baking powder, and salt and mix to incorporate.
4. Put bananas, almond milk, vinegar, and vanilla extract in another bowl and whisk to incorporate.
5. Put the banana mixture into the bowl of the flour mixture and mix well to incorporate it thoroughly.
6. Lightly fold in chocolate chips.
7. Pour batter into the prepared loaf pan.
8. Bake in the oven for 50-60 minutes or until a toothpick inserted into the center comes out clean.
9. Remove the loaf pan from the oven and transfer it to a counter to cool for 10 min.
10. Remove the cake from the pan and shift it onto a platter to cool completely.
11. Cut the cake into serving portions and enjoy.

Blueberry Cobbler

SERVES 4

Ingredients

- ☐ 1 C. self-rising flour
- ☐ ½ C. coconut milk
- ☐ 2 tbsp. coconut oil, melted
- ☐ ¼ C. banana, peeled and mashed
- ☐ 1/2 C. coconut sugar
- ☐ Coarse sugar for sprinkling on top
- ☐ 1½ C. fresh blueberries

Directions

1. For preheating, set your oven to 350°F. Lightly grease an 8-inch baking dish or a cast iron pan.
2. In a bowl, stir together flour with sugar.
3. Add milk, oil, and banana, and stir until combined.
4. Place blueberries at the bottom of the baking dish and top it with flour mixture.
5. Sprinkle the top evenly with coarse sugar.
6. Bake on the middle oven rack uncovered for 45 minutes, until the top is a light golden brown.
7. Enjoy warm. Serve with ice cream or as is.

Apple Crisp

SERVES 10

Ingredients

For the Filling:

- ☐ 4 large apples, peeled and chopped
- ☐ 2 tbsp. fresh apple juice
- ☐ 2 tbsp. water
- ☐ ¼ tsp. ground cinnamon
- ☐ 2 tbsp. maple syrup
- ☐ 1 1/2 tsp. lemon juice

For the Topping:

- ☐ ½ C. quick rolled oats
- ☐ 2 tbsp. walnuts, chopped
- ☐ ¼ C. coconut butter
- ☐ ½ tsp. ground cinnamon

Directions

1. Preheat oven to 350 F degrees. Butter an 8x8 baking dish.
2. In a mixing bowl, add all filling ingredients and gently mix, then transfer to prepared baking dish.
3. In a bowl, add all topping ingredients and mix to incorporate, then spread it over the apples in the baking dish.
4. Bake for 40-45 minutes.
5. Enjoy warm with an ice cream on top.

BERRIES
Tart

 PREP 15 MIN  COOK 12 MIN  SERVES 8

Ingredients

For the Crust:

- ☐ 1 C. blanched almond flour
- ☐ ½ C. dried coconut, shredded
- ☐ ½ C. pecans, chopped
- ☐ 1 tbsp. maple syrup
- ☐ 1/3 C. coconut oil, melted

For the Filling:

- ☐ ½ C. berry or apricot jam
- ☐ 1 C. fresh strawberries, mashed

For the Topping:

- ☐ 1 C. fresh mixed berries (strawberries, blackberries, blueberries)

Directions

1. Preheat your oven to 350°F.
2. Grease an 8-inch tart pot and then line the bottom with a round baking paper.
3. For the crust, add all ingredients to a blender bowl and pulse until a dough forms.
4. Arrange the dough into the prepared tart pan with a removable bottom.
5. With your hands, pat the dough onto the sides and bottom of the pan.
6. Bake for 12-15 minutes and remove it from the oven to cool completely.
7. Meanwhile, mash jam and half of the strawberries in a bowl for filling.
8. Spread the jam mixture over the crust and arrange the fresh mixed berries on top.
9. For the glaze, warm some jam. Use a pastry brush to gently brush the warmed jam over the berries, covering each with a thin layer to create a glossy finish.
10. Refrigerate for at least an hour before enjoying.

NO-BAKE VANILLA
Cheesecake

 PREP 20 MIN COOK 0 MIN  SERVES 12

Ingredients

For the Crust:

- [ ] 1 C. dates, pitted and chopped
- [ ] 1 C. vegan cookies
- [ ] 8 tbsp. coconut oil or vegan butter

For the Filling:

- [ ] 3½ C. cashews, soaked overnight
- [ ] ½ C. coconut oil, melted
- [ ] 8 tbsp. cacao butter
- [ ] 2 tbsp. fresh organic lemon rind, finely grated
- [ ] ¾ C. fresh lemon juice
- [ ] ¾ C. maple syrup
- [ ] 10 drops liquid stevia
- [ ] 1 tsp. vanilla extract
- [ ] Fresh fruit for topping

Directions

1. For the crust: in a food processor, add the dates, almonds, and butter and process until the mixture starts to combine.
2. Transfer the mixture into a greased springform pot and smooth the crust's surface with a spatula.
3. For the filling, melt the cacao butter gently over a water bath and set aside.
4. In the food processor, add the cashews and oil and process to incorporate.
5. Add the remaining ingredients and process until silky smooth.
6. Add melted, cooled cacao butter and blend until well combined.
7. Pour the mixture over the crust and smooth the top with the back of a spatula.
8. Place the tin in the fridge for at least 4 hours to set.
9. Top with fresh fruit. Keep refrigerated. Enjoy.

07 CHAPTER SEVEN

Blissful Sips

Citrus Detox Water

SERVES 3

Ingredients

- ☐ 1 lemon, sliced
- ☐ ½ of cucumber, sliced
- ☐ Fresh mint leaves
- ☐ 2 tbsp. fresh ginger, sliced
- ☐ 6 C. water
- ☐ Ice cubes, as desired

Directions

1. Place fruit, cucumber, ginger, and mint leaves in a large glass jar and pour water over them.
2. Cover the jar with a lid and refrigerate for 2 hours. Enjoy with ice or as is.

Lemonade

SERVES 4

Ingredients

- ☐ ¾ C. fresh squeezed lemon juice
- ☐ 1/2 lemon, sliced
- ☐ 8-10 drops liquid stevia
- ☐ 3½ C. cold water
- ☐ Ice cubes, as desired
- ☐ Mint leaves for garnishing

Directions

1. In a large pitcher, mix the lemon juice and stevia.
2. Add the water and fill the pitcher with ice. Add lemon slices and mint leaves.
3. Enjoy.

Iced Green Tea

SERVES 2

Ingredients

- ☐ 2½ C. hot water (150-175°F)
- ☐ 1 C. fresh mint leaves
- ☐ 2 green tea bags
- ☐ 2 tsp. maple syrup
- ☐ 2 lime slices

Directions

1. Brew tea in a teapot. Add crushed mint.
2. Cover and steep for 5 minutes.
3. Refrigerate for at least 3 hours.
4. Discard the tea bags and divide the tea into serving glasses.
5. Add maple syrup and mix to incorporate.
6. Put in lime slices and ice, and enjoy.

Cranberry Iced Tea

SERVES 7

Ingredients

- ☐ 1¼ C. hot water (150-175°F)
- ☐ 2 dandelion tea bags
- ☐ 6 C. cold water
- ☐ ½ C. unsweetened cranberry juice
- ☐ 6 drops grapefruit juice
- ☐ 6 drops of lemon juice

Directions

1. Add hot water and tea bags to a large glass pitcher. Cover and brew for 10 min.
2. Discard the tea bags and mix in the remaining ingredients.
3. Refrigerate to chill completely before enjoying. Add ice and garnish.

Cold Coffee

SERVES 3

Ingredients

- ☐ 2 C. boiled water
- ☐ 3-4 tbsp. of coffee grounds
- ☐ 1 C. cold unsweetened coconut milk
- ☐ ¼ C. ice cubes

Directions

1. Pour a small amount of hot water into a French press to warm the carafe; discard.
2. Put ground coffee in a carafe. Pour in hot water. Let it stand for 4 minutes.
3. Now, add the cold milk and slowly stir to incorporate it thoroughly.
4. Enjoy over ice cubes.

Ginger Turmeric Shots

SERVES 10

Ingredients

- ☐ 2 oranges, peeled
- ☐ 2 lemons, peeled
- ☐ 8 oz. fresh turmeric, cut into chunks
- ☐ 8 oz. fresh ginger, cut into chunks
- ☐ Pinch of ground black pepper
- ☐ ½ C. water

Directions

1. Add all the ingredients into a blender and blend to form a smooth mixture.
2. Through a cheesecloth, strain the mixture into glasses.
3. Sprinkle with pepper. Enjoy immediately.

Beaten Coffee

SERVES 1

Ingredients

- ☐ ½ tbsp. instant coffee
- ☐ 1½ tbsp. coconut sugar
- ☐ 3 tbsp. boiling water
- ☐ 1 C. oat milk (or nut milk)

Directions

1. In a cup, add the instant coffee, sugar, and hot boiling water and stir briskly for a few minutes until you see a frothy layer on top.
2. In a glass jar or a thermos, shake boiling milk for a few minutes to get the froth on the milk, or use a handheld frother.
3. Pour the foamy milk into the cup containing the coffee. Stir with a spoon.
4. Sprinkle some ground cinnamon. Enjoy.

Pumpkin Latte

SERVES 1

Ingredients

- ☐ 2 tbsp. pure maple syrup
- ☐ 2 tbsp. pumpkin puree
- ☐ ½ tsp. pumpkin pie spice
- ☐ ½ C. unsweetened coconut milk
- ☐ ½ C. strong brewed coffee
- ☐ Whipped coconut cream for topping

Directions

1. Mix the maple syrup, pumpkin puree, and pumpkin pie spice in a small pot over medium heat.
2. Add the coconut milk and cook until just heated through.
3. Take it out of the heat and add in coffee.
4. Pour into a mug and enjoy with whipped cream on top.

Hot Cocoa

SERVES 1

Ingredients

- ☐ 1 tbsp. cacao powder
- ☐ 1 C. full-fat coconut milk
- ☐ 1½ tbsp. vegan chocolate, finely chopped
- ☐ 2-3 drops liquid stevia
- ☐ 1 tbsp. whipped coconut cream

Directions

1. Place coconut milk into a small pot over medium-high heat and cook until boiling.
2. Add cacao powder and chocolate and stir vigorously to form a smooth mixture.
3. Cook for 5 minutes, whisking frequently.
4. Pour the hot chocolate into a serving mug and blend in stevia.
5. Enjoy with the topping of whipped cream.

Black Tea

SERVES 2

Ingredients

- ☐ 2 C. water
- ☐ 2 heaping teaspoons (6g) of black tea leaves
- ☐ 2-3 drops liquid stevia or sweetener of choice

Directions

1. In a small pot, boil water and take it off the heat for a few minutes (200-205F).
2. Add in tea leaves.
3. Immediately cover the pot and let it steep for 3 minutes. If it's too weak, increase the steeping time.
4. Add in stevia and enjoy hot.

Matcha Tea

SERVES 1

Ingredients

- ☐ ½-1 tsp. matcha powder
- ☐ 2 tbsp. hot water
- ☐ 1 C. hot coconut milk
- ☐ 2 tsp. maple syrup

Directions

1. Sift the matcha powder into a mug.
2. Add the hot water and whisk briskly, in an up-and-down motion, until frothy— about 30 seconds.
3. Add the coconut milk and whisk until well combined.
4. Enjoy immediately.

Lemon & Ginger Tea

SERVES 6

Ingredients

- ☐ 6 C. water
- ☐ ½ of lemon, sliced
- ☐ 1-2 (1-inch) piece of fresh ginger, sliced
- ☐ 2 tbsp. maple syrup
- ☐ 1-2 pieces of fresh turmeric, sliced
- ☐ Pinch of ground cinnamon

Directions

1. Add all ingredients over medium-high heat in a pot and cook until boiling.
2. Turn the heat to medium-low and simmer for 10-12 minutes.
3. Strain into a cup and enjoy hot.

Turmeric Latte

SERVES 2

Ingredients

- ☐ 2 C. almond or coconut milk
- ☐ ½ tsp. ground turmeric
- ☐ ½ tsp. fresh or ¼ ground ginger
- ☐ ¼ tsp. ground cinnamon
- ☐ 2 tsp. maple syrup
- ☐ 1 tsp. vanilla extract

Directions

1. Whisk milk, turmeric, cinnamon, & ginger in a small saucepan. Bring to a boil.
2. Lower the heat and simmer for 5 minutes.
3. Turn off the heat and add maple syrup and vanilla extract.
4. Using a strainer, pour the turmeric milk into two cups.

Hot Apple Cider

SERVES 4

Ingredients

- ☐ 2 cinnamon sticks
- ☐ ½ tsp. allspice berries
- ☐ 1 tsp. whole cloves
- ☐ 4 C. fresh apple juice (apple cider)
- ☐ ½ tbsp. orange zest
- ☐ 1-2 tsp. maple syrup

Directions

1. In a large stainless-steel saucepan, pour apple cider and maple syrup.
2. Place cinnamon sticks, cloves, allspice berries, and orange zest in cheesecloth, tie it up, and cook over medium heat for 5-7 minutes. Remove cider from the heat.
3. Discard the spice bundle. Enjoy.

SPICED
Milk Tea

 PREP 10 MIN    COOK 10 MIN   SERVES 6

Ingredients

- [ ] 1 star anise
- [ ] 12 whole cloves
- [ ] 6 whole allspices
- [ ] 2 cinnamon sticks
- [ ] 6 whole white peppercorns
- [ ] 2 tbsp. black tea leaves
- [ ] 2 green cardamom pods, cracked, seeds removed, and pods discarded
- [ ] 1 C. water
- [ ] 4 C. coconut milk
- [ ] 6-8 tsp. agave nectar or coconut sugar

Directions

1. Grind the cardamom, cinnamon stick, and peppercorns with a mortar and pestle or coffee/spice grinder.
2. Bring milk just to a simmer and add ground spice mixture. Reduce heat to low and simmer, stirring occasionally, for 3-5 minutes to infuse flavors.
3. Meanwhile, bring water to a boil and add tea.
4. Let it steep for 3 minutes.
5. Pour tea through a fine-mesh sieve into the hot milk mixture and cook over low heat for 1 minute.
6. Strain the tea into serving mugs and add in agave nectar.
7. Enjoy hot.

08

CHAPTER EIGHT

Sip & Smile Smoothies

Apple & Banana Smoothie

SERVES 2

Ingredients

- [ ] 1 frozen banana, peeled and sliced
- [ ] 1 green apple, peeled, cored and chopped
- [ ] 1¼ C. unsweetened almond milk
- [ ] ½ C. ice cubes
- [ ] Sprinkle of cinnamon

Directions

1. Put bananas and remaining ingredients into a high-power blender and process to form a smooth and creamy smoothie.
2. Sprinkle with ground cinnamon.
3. Enjoy immediately.

Kiwi & Melon Smoothie

SERVES 2

Ingredients

- [ ] 2 kiwi fruit, peeled and chopped
- [ ] 2 C. cantaloupe melon, chopped
- [ ] ½ tsp. fresh ginger, chopped
- [ ] 1½ scoops vegan protein powder
- [ ] ½ tbsp. fresh lime juice
- [ ] ¼ C. ice cubes
- [ ] Mint leaves for granishing

Directions

1. Put kiwis and remaining ingredients into a high-power blender and process to form a smooth and creamy smoothie.
2. Garnish and enjoy immediately.

Raspberry & Banana Smoothie 🍴

SERVES 2

Ingredients

- [ ] 2 C. frozen raspberries
- [ ] 1 small banana, peeled and sliced
- [ ] 1½ C. unsweetened almond milk
- [ ] ¼ C. ice cubes

Directions

1. Put raspberries and remaining ingredients into a high-power blender and process to form a smooth and creamy smoothie.
2. Enjoy immediately.

Blueberry & Banana Smoothie 🍴

SERVES 3

Ingredients

- [ ] 1 C. plain vegan unsweetened coconut milk yogurt
- [ ] 1C. fresh or frozen blueberries
- [ ] 1 large banana, sliced
- [ ] ½ C. coconut milk
- [ ] ½ C. ice

Directions

1. Put strawberries and remaining ingredients into a high-power blender and process to form a smooth and creamy smoothie.
2. Enjoy immediately.

96

Raspberry & Peach Smoothie

SERVES 2

Ingredients

- [ ] 1 C. fresh or frozen peaches
- [ ] ½ C. frozen raspberries
- [ ] ¼ tsp. vanilla extract
- [ ] ½ C. 100% pure pomegranate juice

Directions

1. Add peach, vanilla extract, and ½ C. ice cubes to a blender & blend until smooth.
2. Pour the smoothie out evenly into two glasses and rinse the blender.
3. Add raspberries and pomegranate juice to the blender and blend until smooth.
4. Carefully pour over the peach layer in the glasses and garnish with fresh fruit.

Pineapple Smoothie

SERVES 2

Ingredients

- [ ] 1½ C. pineapple, chopped
- [ ] Half of a banana
- [ ] 1 tsp. ground turmeric
- [ ] 1 tsp. chia seeds
- [ ] ½ C. coconut water

Directions

1. Put pineapple and remaining ingredients into a high-power blender and process to form a smooth and creamy smoothie.
2. Garnish with pineapple and sprinkle with chia seeds.
3. Enjoy immediately.

Blueberry & Spinach Smoothie

SERVES 2

Ingredients

- ☐ 2 C. fresh spinach
- ☐ ¾ C. frozen blueberries
- ☐ 4-6 drops liquid stevia
- ☐ 1½ C. unsweetened almond milk
- ☐ 1 tsp. flax seeds for garnishing

Directions

1. Put spinach and remaining ingredients into a high-power blender and process to form a smooth and creamy smoothie.
2. Sprinkle with flax seeds.
3. Enjoy immediately.

Avocado & Mint Smoothie

SERVES 2

Ingredients

- ☐ 1 avocado, peeled, pitted and chopped
- ☐ 12-14 fresh mint leaves
- ☐ 2 tbsp. fresh lime juice
- ☐ ½ tsp. vanilla extract
- ☐ 1½ C. unsweetened almond milk
- ☐ ¼ C. ice cubes

Directions

1. Add the avocado and all the ingredients to a blender and blend until smooth.
2. Pour the smoothie out evenly into two glasses. Garnish with mint and lime.
3. Enjoy.

Cucumber & Parsley Smoothie 🍴

SERVES 4

Ingredients

- ☐ 2 C. cucumber, peeled and chopped
- ☐ 2 C. fresh parsley
- ☐ 1 Celery stick, chopped
- ☐ 1 (1-inch) piece of fresh ginger root
- ☐ 2 tbsp. fresh lemon juice
- ☐ 4-6 drops liquid stevia
- ☐ 2 C. chilled water

Directions

1. Add cucumber and the remaining ingredients in a high-power blender and blend until smooth.
2. Enjoy chilled.

Green Veggies Smoothie 🍴

SERVES 3

Ingredients

- ☐ 1 C. fresh spinach
- ☐ ¼ C. broccoli florets, chopped
- ☐ ¼ C. green apple, chopped
- ☐ ½ of small green bell pepper, seeded
- ☐ 3 tbsp. agave syrup
- ☐ 2 C. chilled water

Directions

1. Put spinach, apple, broccoli, and remaining ingredients into a high-power blender and process until smooth.
2. Garnish with lime wedge.
3. Enjoy immediately.

MEAL *planner*

	BREAKFAST	LUNCH	DINNER
DAY 1	Blueberry Oatmeal	Veggie Avocado Salad	Kidney Beans Curry
DAY 2	Matcha Pancakes	Stuffed Bell Peppers	Barley & Lentil Stew
DAY 3	Nuts & Seeds Porridge	Asparagus Soup	Tofu Pad Thai
DAY 4	Avocado & Mint Smoothie	Avocado & Veggie Tortilla Wraps	Beans & Mushroom Chili
DAY 5	Apple Cinnamon Oatmeal	Homemade Ratatouille	Rice & Veggie Paella
DAY 6	Oats, Nuts & Seeds Muesli	Veggie Tacos	Chickpeas & Tomato Soup
DAY 7	Green Veggies Smoothie	Apple & Walnut Salad	Eggplant Parmesan
DAY 8	Tofu & Veggie Scramble	Corn Chowder	Split Pea & Carrot Soup
DAY 9	Eggless Tomato Omelet	Tofu Broccoli Stir Fry	Pasta with Mushrooms
DAY 10	Banana Muffins	Vegetarian Pie	Beans & Barley Soup
DAY 11	Buckwheat Porridge	Chickpeas Falafels	Kidney Beans Curry
DAY 12	Matcha Pancakes	Pasta with Mushrooms	Black Beans Enchiladas
DAY 13	Apple & Date Cookies	Mushroom & Spinach Soup	Lentil & Potato Stew
DAY 14	Chia Seed Pudding	Pomegranate & Couscous Salad	Pasta & Carrot Soup

DAY 15	Zucchini Bread	Stuffed Sweet Potatoes	Beans & Mushroom Chili
DAY 16	Blueberry Oatmeal	Chickpeas Sandwich	Pumpkin Curry
DAY 17	Apple Cinnamon Oatmeal	Tomato Pizza	Lentil & Squash Soup
DAY 18	Broccoli Quiche	Chickpeas Falafels	Mushroom & Spinach Soup
DAY 19	Banana Waffles	Tofu Pad Thai	Roasted Brussels Sprouts
DAY 20	Granola & Berries Yogurt Bowl	Veggie Lettuce Wraps	Pasta with Mushrooms
DAY 21	Green Smoothie Bowl	Tomato Soup	Cauliflower & Potato Curry
DAY 22	Oats, Nuts & Seeds Muesli	Cabbage Rolls	Sweet Potato & Chickpeas Stew
DAY 23	Tofu & Veggie Scramble	Cauliflower Soup	Black Beans Enchiladas
DAY 24	Mushroom & Avocado Toast	Vegan Mushroom Burger	Rice & Veggie Paella
DAY 25	Zucchini Bread	Chickpeas & Veggie Salad	Vegetable Soup
DAY 26	Blueberry Oatmeal	Tofu & Veggie Lettuce Wraps	Veggie Fried Rice
DAY 27	Mushroom & Avocado Toast	Rice & Lentil Loaf	Cauliflower & Potato Curry
DAY 28	Veggies Frittata	Cabbage Soup	Black Beans Enchiladas
DAY 29	Buckwheat Porridge	Veggies Sandwich	Beans & Barley Soup
DAY 30	Spiced Quinoa Porridge	Pumpkin Soup	Vegan Mushroom Burger

GROCERY
shopping list

◯ Vegetables:

- zucchini
- yellow squash
- eggplant
- mushrooms
- green beans
- bell pepper
- broccoli
- broccolini
- cauliflower

- pumpkin
- Brussels sprouts
- potato
- sweet potato
- butternut squash
- sugar snap peas
- mung bean sprouts
- olives
- celery

- corn
- radish
- cucumber
- asparagus
- carrot
- cabbage
- beets
- tomato

◯ FRESH HERBS:

- onion
- scallion
- lettuce
- baby greens
- garlic
- capers
- spinach
- dill

- basil
- thyme
- rosemary
- mint
- oregano
- jalapeño pepper
- kale
- chives

- lemon
- lime
- cilantro
- parsley
- ginger
- turmeric

FRUITS 8 BERRIES:

- blueberries
- raspberries
- strawberries
- blackberries
- cranberries
- cherries
- kiwi

- pineapple
- mango
- apple
- melon
- grapes
- peach
- pears

- coconut
- banana
- pomegranate
- dates
- orange
- grapefruit
- avocado

Grains 8 Legumes:

- oats
- buckwheat groats
- quinoa
- bulgur wheat
- barley
- couscous
- vegan rice noodles

- wild rice
- brown rice
- lentils
- split peas
- vegan pasta
- vegan noodles
- red kidney beans

- black-eyed peas
- chickpeas
- white beans
- black beans
- pinto beans

Nuts 8 Seeds:

- pecans
- walnuts
- almonds
- peanuts
- cashews

- hazelnuts
- pine nuts
- chia seeds
- sunflower seeds
- pumpkin seeds

- sesame seeds
- flaxseeds
- flaxseed meal

SEASONINGS & SPICES:

- salt
- garlic powder
- onion powder
- black pepper
- cayenne pepper
- paprika
- red chili powder
- red pepper flakes
- sumac
- turmeric
- cumin
- coriander
- cinnamon
- ginger
- nutmeg
- cardamom
- curry powder
- Italian seasoning
- pumpkin pie spice
- allspice berries
- peppercorns
- star anise
- whole allspices
- whole cloves
- thyme
- oregano
- rosemary
- marjoram
- bay leaf

MILK, BUTTER, OIL & OTHER:

- almond milk
- coconut milk
- soy milk
- oat milk
- coconut yogurt
- coconut water
- soy yogurt
- coconut cream
- almond butter
- peanut butter
- vegan mayonnaise
- vegan butter
- veg. parmesan cheese
- veg. mozzarella cheese
- vegan ice cream
- palm shortening
- non-stick baking spray
- coconut oil
- olive oil
- canola oil
- vegetable oil
- peanut oil
- sesame oil
- whole-wheat flour
- almond flour
- coconut flour
- arrowroot flour
- spelt flour
- buckwheat flour
- oat flour
- chickpea flour
- tapioca starch
- cornmeal
- baking soda
- baking powder
- Erythritol
- maple syrup
- applesauce
- agave nectar
- stevia powder
- liquid stevia
- vanilla extract
- vegan protein powder
- Dijon mustard
- coconut flakes
- vegan pizza dough
- vegan bread
- corn tortillas
- matcha powder
- tofu
- nutritional yeast
- tahini
- hummus
- nutritional yeast
- soy sauce
- v. Worcestershire sauce
- agar agar
- marinara sauce
- ketchup
- balsamic vinegar
- white vinegar
- apple cider vinegar
- vegetable broth
- cacao powder
- coffee powder
- vegan chocolate
- black tea leaves
- dandelion tea
- green tea

ACKNOWLEDGMENTS

As we reach the conclusion of this book, let's pause for a moment to ponder the path we have traveled together. We have delved into the fundamentals of a plant-based diet and the impact of adopting one, discussed the different aspects of a plant-based diet, and uncovered delectable recipes that feed not just the body but also the soul. We have discussed common obstacles and offered remedies to ensure your shift to a plant-based way of living is seamless and pleasurable.

You now possess the information and resources needed to adopt a plant-based diet. You understand how consuming plant-based foods influences your overall health and happiness. You have discovered the art of preparing nourishing and delicious meals. Your connection with food has the potential to be altered, helping you move towards reaching your health objectives.

The adventure continues further. With the knowledge, it's time to dive in and apply it. Begin integrating the recipes and advice from this book into your life. Explore new ingredients, test meal schedules, and pay attention to how your body reacts to these adjustments. Remember that this journey is unique, so discovering what suits you best is the key.

I encourage you to adhere to this lifestyle choice, even when faced with obstacles. The advantages of adopting a plant-based diet are vast and impactful, ranging from increased vitality and improved digestion to a reinforced immune system and an enhanced overall state of health. Embrace this path with an open mind, heart, and willingness to absorb knowledge and evolve.

Remember, every step you take towards a plant-based lifestyle is a step towards a healthier, more compassionate world. Happy cooking and happy eating!

Thank you!

If this book has been helpful to you, please share your thoughts with others on Amazon by leaving a review. A positive review not only supports me as the author and creator but also spreads the message of healthy living to a wider audience.

Thank you for allowing me to accompany you on this journey. Here's to a joyful, healthier, and more lively you!

REFERENCES

Harvard T.H. Chan School of Public Health. (2021). Why plant-based diets are good for health. Retrieved from https://www.hsph.harvard.edu/nutritionsource/healthy-eating-plate/

MD Anderson Cancer Center. (2019). 5 benefits of a plant-based diet. Retrieved from https://www.mdanderson.org

Oxford Academic. American Society for Nutrition. (2018). Healthy plant-based diets are associated with a lower risk of all-cause mortality in US adults. The Journal of Nutrition. Retrieved from https://academic.oup.com

American Heart Association. (2023). How does plant-forward (plant-based) eating benefit your health? Retrieved from https://www.heart.org

Kahleova, H., Levin, S., & Barnard, N. (2017). Cardio-metabolic benefits of plant-based diets. Nutrients, 9(8), 848. https://doi.org/10.3390/nu9080848

Harvard Health Publishing. (2024). What is a plant-based diet and why should you try it? Retrieved from https://www.health.harvard.edu

Stanford Report. (2021). Embracing a plant-based diet. Retrieved from https://news.stanford.edu/

Medical News Today. (2018). Nutrition 2018: New data confirm health benefits of plant-based diet. Retrieved from https://www.medicalnewstoday.com

Parkview Health (2023). Transitioning to a plant-based diet – tips and tricks. https://www.parkview.com/

Discover Magazine. (2020). What science says about the health benefits of plant-based diets. Retrieved from https://www.discovermagazine.com

Made in United States
Orlando, FL
20 November 2024

54148350R10059